THE READING–WRITING WORKSHOP:

Getting Started

Designed by Jacqueline Swensen
Cover design by Vincent Ceci
Cover art by Anna V. Walker
Interior illustration by Rick Brown

ISBN 0-590-49167-9

12 11 10 9 8 7 6 5 4 3   4 5/9

Printed in the U.S.A.

*With grateful appreciation to our students,
who inspired us, our colleagues,
who believed in us, and most of all to our families,
who encouraged and supported us.*

NORMA AND PAULA

THE READING–WRITING WORKSHOP:
Getting Started

Norma R. Jackson
with
Paula L. Pillow

SCHOLASTIC
PROFESSIONAL BOOKS

NEW YORK • TORONTO • LONDON • AUCKLAND • SYDNEY

Contents

4. ORGANIZING THE CLASSROOM FOR A READING-WRITING WORKSHOP

5. READING-WRITING WORKSHOP LESSONS INTRODUCTION

Continued

Introduction

Paula Pillow and I began to explore the possibilities of implementing a Reading-Writing Workshop after attending a whole-language seminar at which Kenneth Goodman was the keynote speaker. We were interested in the ideas we were hearing and began discussing ways to try them out in our own classes. Throughout the two-day seminar various whole-language advocates kept referring to several "must read" books. (These are included in the bibliography.) So Paula and I agreed we would purchase different books and then exchange them. What began as a sensible partnership would soon grow into a wonderful career-changing adventure!

Over the next few months, whenever we read some eye-opening comment or suggestion in our books, we'd call the other one to share our insights. We usually agreed on our goals but not always on how to achieve them. Sometimes we took turns dredging up all the possible reasons that an idea might not work. Other times one of us would come up with a great idea that the other one would elaborate and refine to make even better. In either case, it was a win-win situation. Whether our talks enhanced an idea or made us rethink it, we'd always come away from our discussions with a broader view.

This book grew out of our triumphs and frustrations. Even after reading more than a dozen books on the whole-language approach by well-known authors, we still did not find one that outlined how to set up and sustain a Reading-Writing Workshop. Therefore, we decided to do it ourselves! While I became the primary writer, the ideas were a collaborative effort.

At first we felt that our publishing goal was a little grandiose. After all, we had been involved in our program for only two years. However, the fact that we were so close to the learning process put us in an excellent position to offer suggestions to other teachers who were interested in setting up a Reading-Writing Workshop. We are now in our third year of implementing the Workshop. Each year we have used the same basic strategies outlined in this book, while adjusting them to our different students' needs.

We hope that this book will make your process of getting started a little easier. We know you will still face your own struggles. Debate the merits of each suggestion as it applies to your teaching situation. Then refine, reshape, and elaborate the ideas to create your own Reading-Writing Workshop. It is an adventure that is truly worth the effort!

Good luck and best wishes,
Norma Jackson

CHAPTER ONE

THE READING– WRITING WORKSHOP: WHAT AND WHY

The Reading-Writing Workshop is much like a road map you'd take with you on a vacation. On a trip, you might decide to spend half your time in the mountains and half your time at the ocean; you might take a side trip to a desert village or visit sights along the main highway. Without diminishing your power to choose, the map clearly shows you your options. Therefore, it helps you plan a trip that best fits your needs and interests, while always keeping your final destination in sight.

As I move toward integrating rather than isolating language arts skills, the Reading-Writing Workshop acts as my road map. It provides a setting that allows my students to have meaningful experiences reading, writing, listening, and speaking as they respond to literature. However, it is flexible enough that both my students and I retain our power to make choices.

My students spend quality time each day on self-selected reading and writing activities in their areas of interest. Furthermore, the Workshop allows students to share responsibility for their own learning.

At the same time, the Workshop gives me opportunities to use my instructional time to the maximum benefit of my students. Within its daily time frame I am able to work with students both individually and in small groups, to present whole-class skills lessons, and to introduce students to a variety of authors, illustrators, genres, and themes.

There are three distinct parts of the Reading-Writing Workshop—Independent Work, Literature Focus lessons, and Skills lessons. These parts provide a structured framework for the Workshop. Within this framework, further structure is provided by the basic procedures that apply to whichever task the student is involved in, and by evaluation methods that you can easily adapt to meet the grading requirements of your state and district. Even the Literature Focus and Skills lessons can, to some degree, be planned and outlined well in advance.

While the Workshop offers structure, it remains quite flexible. Students choose for themselves which literature they will read, they respond to their reading based on their own experiences, and they determine the topics and styles of writing they will use.

As the teacher, you have flexibility too. You may vary both the order and the length of each of the three Workshop parts. Before too long you will base your Literature Focus lessons and Skills lessons not on a predetermined schedule but on topics and problems that arise during Independent Work. In short, the students—and you—have a map that allows all of you to explore new ideas and projects without the fear of getting lost.

The ultimate goal of the Reading-Writing Workshop is to let your students' needs and interests shape the learning process. Does that sound a bit risky and unsettling? I certainly had misgivings when I began to develop the Workshop. For many years I had relied heavily on the wisdom of a basal manual to know when and how to present skills. Now I was basing my lessons primarily on the observed needs of my students. This was scary! What if I skipped a skill? How would I know what my students needed to learn next? How could I evaluate their progress and support my observations to parents?

At first, the Workshop approach seemed like an invitation to chaos and a challenge to document (and like it or not, documentation is a very real part of education), but as I took that first leap of faith I found that offering my students many experiences with real language enabled them to discover patterns and make generalizations for themselves.

This does not mean that children should be left entirely to their own devices to figure out our complicated language system. Whole-class skills lessons and individual guidance are an integral part of the Workshop. But this instruction takes place in response to students' needs. My classroom is much like a self-checking game. When my students' progress slows down, it is easy to see that they need something. This need becomes the focus of my next lesson(s). By taking the same positive role that a parent takes in teaching a young child to speak, I now lead, rather than force, my students to make meaningful connections between listening, speaking, reading, and writing.

Like I did, you may feel nervous

about breaking away from the basal text and embarking on your own Reading-Writing Workshop. I hope that this book will help to give you the confidence that I had to acquire through trial and error.

Chapter 2 outlines the organization of the Workshop and briefly describes the three parts. Chapter 3 goes into detail about the varied tasks involved, the interactions between students and their peers and between students and teacher, and methods of evaluating students' progress. Chapter 4 suggests the kind of classroom layout that is desirable for a successful Workshop. Chapter 5 describes the kinds of lessons that can play a natural and effective role in the Workshop, and provides sample guides for 20 basic lessons that will enable you to launch a Reading-Writing Workshop in your own classroom.

As you start your Workshop you will undoubtedly want to modify many of the details in this book to suit your own and your students' needs. I have described my own experiences so that you can see the practices of a Workshop that is already in operation. But no matter whether you follow or change these practices, you and your students will be embarking on a voyage of discovery and excitement.

CHAPTER TWO

HOW THE WORKSHOP WORKS

My Reading-Writing Workshop takes place every day for 1 hour to 2 ½ hours, depending on other scheduling requirements. It consists of three parts that can vary from day to day, both in length and in order of presentation. These three parts are Independent Work, Literature Focus, and Skills.

Although Independent Work is in many ways the most important of these three, and certainly the one to which I usually allot the most time, you cannot introduce it until students are familiar with the tasks involved. You prepare them for these tasks by means of Literature Focus and Skills lessons.

Literature Focus

(30–45 minutes)

While there are some similarities between Literature Focus lessons and traditional basal reading activities, for the most part, their purposes are very different. Traditionally, manuals for basals provide activities that set the stage for reading, review vocabulary, and highlight particular reading skills. But with the Literature Focus lessons, the emphasis is on developing a deeper appreciation of the literature selection.

This "appreciation" might include sharing information about an author's life, comparing one author's style to another's, or investigating the characteristics of tall tales or mysteries.

The first six Literature Focus lessons (included in this book) cover the basic reading tasks involved in Independent Work, from Choosing Books to Supporting Opinions. From then on, however, I use this block of time for broader and more creative purposes.

Literature Focus can be to students what a travel brochure is to an avid traveler. It can heighten their awareness of the world of books and invite them to do further exploring on their own. In this period I may introduce my students to a particular book, an author or illustrator, a style of writing, a curriculum-based theme, or a broad theme in literature (friendship,

treasures, journeys, etc.).

Sometimes I read an entire book aloud. Sometimes I read only the passages that demonstrate the technique or idea on which I want to focus. Other times I present a thought-provoking idea and then let my students explore it on their own or in small groups. For example, during our social studies unit on geography we discussed literary maps. After completing a literary map of *The True Story of the 3 Little Pigs* by Jon Scieszka, each group of two to four students read a different book and prepared its own literary map.

Finding a way to bind stories together with a common thread is at the core of the Literature Focus. Whether the focus is on a particular author, illustrator, curriculum-based theme, or literature theme, my goal is to help students make connections between literature and life.

Skills

(15–30 minutes)

The first ten Skills lessons (included in this book) cover the basic process writing tasks involved in Independent Work, from choosing a topic to publishing (preparing a writing project for other students to read). Having completed these, I broaden the focus to cover all language skills, whether related primarily to writing or to reading.

Ideally, I use this block of time to present language strategies that grow directly from my students' needs. Realistically, there are occasions when I have to present specific skills mandated by state or district objectives.

Like most teachers, I have to administer rigorous state and national tests and therefore need to familiarize my students with the test format (which often presents skills in ways that are peculiar to the test and not necessarily natural to reading and writing). I do this during Skills time. I've found that by purposely setting this type of instruction apart, I can avoid compromising the natural development and interaction between reading, writing, listening, and speaking that occurs throughout the rest of my Reading-Writing Workshop.

When I teach a test-taking strategy, I always try to link it to my students' long-term needs first, and then to the test. For example, I might read a short passage from a book and ask, "What did the word *pummel* mean in this selection? *Pummel* is a new word to us. How did you know what it meant? (We used the words around it to help us figure out the meaning.) This is how you might see this skill on a test. . . ."

Still, most of my Skills lessons evolve from needs I observe in my classroom. I use the lessons to present general strategies such as how to make inferences from details given in a story, or to present specific skills such as defining and identifying prepositions. I always try to relate these skills back to reading, writing, listening, or speaking. I've found that Skills lessons are most effective when linked to real literature, and so I often spin them off from the Literature Focus selection. For example, following a Skills lesson on prepositions I read *When I Was Young In the Mountains*, made a class list of prepositional phrases used in the book (there are more than 50), and discussed how the author used those phrases as an elaboration technique.

Independent Work

(60–90 minutes)

The first six Literature Focus lessons and the ten Skills lessons (included in this book) are prerequisites to working independently in the Reading-Writing Workshop. The Literature Focus lessons introduce the procedures and skills needed to complete the students' Reading Contract responsibilities. The Skills lessons present the process-writing strategies that are used during Independent Work.

Since these procedures and strategies are the backbone of Independent Work, introducing and refining them will consume a large portion of my Reading-Writing Workshop at first. Therefore, as

I take my students through these basic lessons, I only introduce short periods of Independent Work. Once they have mastered all of the basic lessons, they work independently for the full 60-to-90 minute block of time while I meet with individuals or small groups.

I display the following Flow Chart bulletin board to direct the sequence of my students' independent work. (Reproducible Flow Chart pieces are on pages 126–134.)

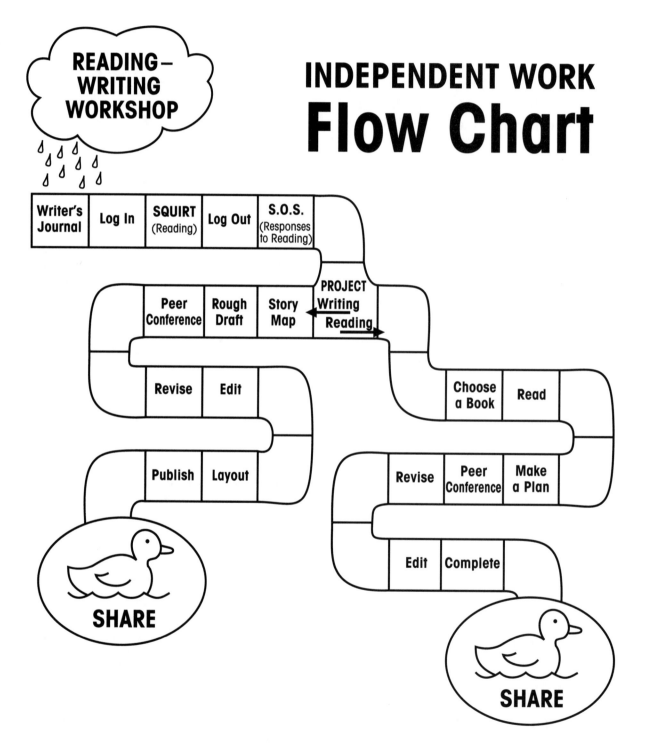

Let's take a closer look at each step in this chart. (In the following description, the basic Literature Focus and Skills lessons that support each step are noted as LF or SL followed by the lesson number.) You will find a full exploration of each step in subsequent chapters.

The first section of the chart, along the top row, is standard for all students every day:

▶ They begin their Independent Work time by recording feelings, impressions, observations, and so on in their Writer's Journals (SL 1).

▶ Then they move on to reading—for which I use the term SQUIRT (Sustained Quiet Uninterrupted Independent Reading Time) from Beverly Kobrin's Eyeopeners! They choose their own books (LF 1) and read independently, keeping a log of their choices (LF 2).

▶ Students respond to their reading by providing what I call S.O.S. (Summary/Opinion & Support). In other words, they write a summary and a reasoned appraisal of what they have read (LF 3 through 5). Other basic requirements for this reading time are covered by each student's Reading Contract (LF 6).

During the second section of Independent Work, students either begin or continue working on a Writing Project or a Reading Project—hence the fork in the flow chart.

As you follow each project on the chart, note that both include Peer Conference (SL 8). At this stage, students show their work-in-progress to two other students for comment.

▶ On a Writing Project, students follow all the steps, from choosing a topic to presenting (publishing) the completed work, in a form that fellow students can read (SL 2 through 10). Writing topics may grow out of entries in students' journals, be inspired by students' reading, or even come from an unfamiliar field that students want to research.

▶ A Reading Project involves more than simply reading and reporting on a book. It is a creative way in which students can share a book they've read—such as a puppet show retelling the plot or a wanted poster describing a character. (LF 7 through 10 present other strategies that students can apply to a wide variety of books.)

When students finish their projects, they share them with the class. I use further Literature Focus and Skills lessons throughout the year to introduce different book-sharing strategies and publishing formats. I've found it helpful to create a project poster or bulletin board on which to record ideas students might want to try (see page 20). I add new ideas to the poster as I introduce them. In addition, many of my students modify and invent techniques of their own.

READING PROJECT
▼▼▼▼▼▼▼▼▼▼▼▼▼▼▼▼

Puppet Show	Play
Wanted Poster	Diorama
Book Jacket	Book Map
Literary Letter	Board Game
Travel Brochure	Interview

WRITING PROJECTS
▼▼▼▼▼▼▼▼▼▼▼▼▼▼▼▼▼

Shape Book	Poem
Pop-Up Book	Poster
Newspaper	Letter
Mini-Book	Research
Song Lyrics	Riddles

Lesson Outlines and Plans

Independent Work does not require a lesson plan in the usual sense of the word. I use this time to keep track of my students' progress, and you will find a step-by-step discussion of these strategies in the following chapter.

For the Literature Focus and Skills lessons, I rely on just two documentary resources: a Reading-Writing Workshop Notebook and a book of Lesson Plan Forms.

READING-WRITING WORKSHOP NOTEBOOK
This contains the outlines of my Literature Focus and Skills lessons. I write each outline on a separate piece of notebook paper. Since I often repeat the same lesson using different literature as the focus, I keep a list of applicable literature on the back of the page, as shown below.

Note that I give each outline a general category heading (in this case, Literal

---

LITERAL COMPREHENSION
▼▼▼▼▼▼▼▼▼▼▼▼▼▼▼▼▼▼▼▼

ACTIVITY 1 (Sequence)
Travel Diaries

1. Brainstorm characteristics of a travel diary.

2. Create a diary describing a trip. Include name of place, location, description, people, and an account of activities.

LITERATURE
▼▼▼▼▼▼▼▼▼▼

The Angry Moon

Arrow to the Sun

Hey, Al

The Polar Express

Where the Wild Things Are

Comprehension) and an Activity number that shows the order in which I plan to teach each lesson under that heading.

I divide my Notebook into tabbed sections, one for each heading. The headings I use are:

LITERATURE FOCUS
▶ Getting Started (Lessons 1–6)
▶ Author Studies
▶ Literature Themes
▶ Reading Project Ideas

SKILLS
▶ Getting Started (Lessons 1–10)
▶ Literal Comprehension
▶ Inferred Meanings
▶ Writing Mechanics
▶ Spelling Generalizations
▶ Types of Writing (Descriptive, How-To, Narrative, Compare and Contrast, Persuasive)
▶ Writing Project Ideas

I find it possible to file any lesson topic under one or other of these headings. You, of course, may find it practical to use more, fewer, or different headings for your own Notebook.

LESSON PLAN FORMS
I use preprinted forms that include a summary of the Independent Work Flow Chart and that allow me to fill in brief reminders of the Literature Focus and Skills lessons, as you can see in the sample below. On this form, I simply refer to the lesson by strategy and activity number. I can easily modify and reuse a lesson without having to rewrite it in my Workshop Notebook. I keep the Lesson Plan Forms in a separate book.

Lesson Plans: Norma Jackson Week of _Oct. 15-19_

Note: All teacher's editions and unit notebooks are located on the small bookshelf beside

W O R K S H O P	Monday	Tuesday	Wednesday
	Reading-Writing Workshop: As students arrive they will immediately begin daily independent tasks from the Flow Chart (Writer's Journal, Log In, SQUIRT, Log Out, S.O.S.). Then they will continue working on their individual reading or writing project following the sequence outlined on the Flow Chart. **Teacher:** Quick-Check (Substitute teacher walks around and monitors.) Reading-Writing Conferences (Weekly Conference Schedule attached)		
L I T E R A T U R	Reading-Writing Workshop Notebook Obj. _Sequence_ Strategy _Literal Comprehension_ Lesson _1_ _Write whole class travel diary for Where the Wild Things Are_	Reading-Writing Workshop Notebook Obj. _Sequence_ Strategy _Literal Comprehension_ Lesson _1_ _Work in small groups. Use self-selected literature._	Reading-Writing Workshop Notebook Obj. _Sequence_ Strategy _Literal Comprehension_ Lesson _1_ _Finish diaries._

Time Management

You'll use the Flow Chart bulletin board as a management system for structuring your students' Independent Work time. Add each section to the Flow Chart as students are ready to work on those tasks, or else display the entire chart but keep the individual tasks covered until you've introduced them. Post-it™ notes or small cutout shapes will do the job.

You'll find reproducible parts of the Flow Chart at the end of this book. (For my class, I reproduce them on blue paper to make my *"Flow"* Chart look like water. Then I "stock" my flowing river with small fish and laminate the pieces for durability.) While keeping to the sequence, you can change the shape of the chart to fit your bulletin board space by repositioning the curved joints.

FLEXIBLE SCHEDULING

Your scheduling needs will change as you move from the beginning stages of the Reading-Writing Workshop to full implementation. These pie charts (see below) show how the proportions of the three components will shift.

The total time you spend on the Reading-Writing Workshop each day can be flexible. Depending on class requirements and other circumstances, my own Workshop may vary from a minimum of 60 minutes to a maximum of 2 ½ hours.

The order in which you present the three components may also differ from

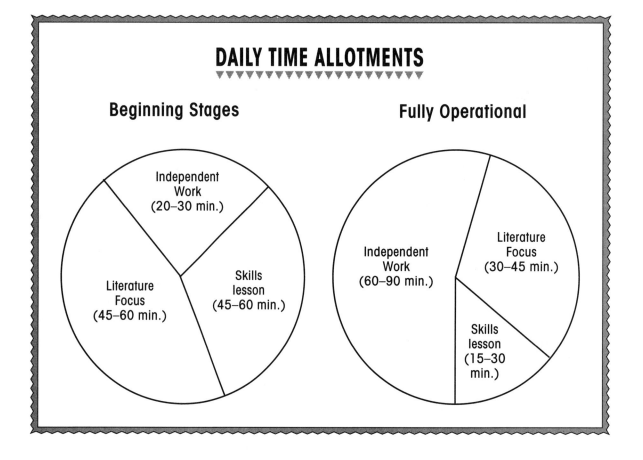

DAILY TIME ALLOTMENTS

Beginning Stages

Independent Work (20–30 min.)

Literature Focus (45–60 min.)

Skills lesson (45–60 min.)

Fully Operational

Independent Work (60–90 min.)

Literature Focus (30–45 min.)

Skills lesson (15–30 min.)

SAMPLE LESSON PLAN

	MONDAY	TUESDAY	WEDNESDAY	THURSDAY	FRIDAY
W O R K S H O P	Independent Work: None.	Independent Work: SQUIRT for 10 minutes.	Independent Work: SQUIRT for 10 minutes.	Independent Work: SQUIRT for 15 minutes.	Independent Work: SQUIRT for 15 minutes.
L I T E R A T U R E F O C U S	Literature Focus: Lesson 1— Choosing Books.	Literature Focus: Lesson 2— Introduce Writer's Journal. Prepare covers.	Literature Focus: Lesson 2— Writer's Journal. Make first entry. Add Journal to Independent Work tasks.	Literature Focus: Lesson 3— Summarize. Model using *Pigs Might Fly.*	Literature Focus: Lesson 3— Summarize. Model using *Arthur's Pen Pal.*
S K I L L S L E S S O N	Skills Lesson 1: Independent Reading. Prepare Reading Folders. Add Log In, SQUIRT, Log Out to Flow Chart.	Skills Lesson 2: Writing Topics. Prepare Writing Folders. Complete "Brainstorms" worksheet.	Skills Lesson 3: Introduction Writing Process. Read *The Carrot Spread.* Discuss author background.	Skills Lesson 4: Writing Process. Discuss steps. Complete "Writing Process Pencil" worksheet.	Skills Lesson 5: Story Mapping. Model story map for *Amelia Bedelia.*

one day to the next. For example, on days when the children go off to special classes early in the morning (music, art, physical education, computer, etc.), I schedule the Skills lesson first. When the students return, they begin Independent Work and finish the morning with Literature Focus. On other days, I may start with Independent Work time. Some of the variations I use are on page 24.

ONE STEP AT A TIME

The first year I began my Reading-Writing Workshop I tried to do too much too fast. In fact, if it hadn't been for my students' enthusiasm and excitement, I might have given up. However, the motivation and achievement this approach fosters is well worth the time and effort it will take to work out the bugs and create your own Reading-Writing Workshop, customized to fit

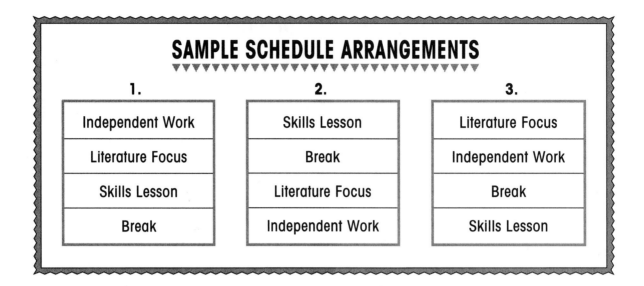

SAMPLE SCHEDULE ARRANGEMENTS

1.

Independent Work
Literature Focus
Skills Lesson
Break

2.

Skills Lesson
Break
Literature Focus
Independent Work

3.

Literature Focus
Independent Work
Break
Skills Lesson

your special situation. Just remember to take it one step at a time. If you find yourself feeling overwhelmed, concentrate on either the Literature Focus or the Skills lessons. Add the second category when you feel on top of the first.

Since there is no sharp division between reading and writing, in my own Workshop I use the names Literature Focus and Skills Lessons for the latter two parts. If you introduce the Workshop into your classroom — as I hope you will! — you may use my names or any others you find appropriate.

CHAPTER THREE

KEEPING TRACK OF STUDENTS

Initially, one of my greatest concerns about implementing a Reading-Writing Workshop was the seeming lack of student accountability. If students were reading literature they selected themselves, how could I evaluate their comprehension? How would I know if they were really reading the words, or simply retelling a familiar story? What if I had never read the books they chose? How could I fairly evaluate a creative effort such as writing? What would I say to parents? How could I explain a student's progress to a parent who rarely saw a worksheet brought home?

As I began attending literacy conferences and whole language workshops, and reading books by the educators who had pioneered these techniques, I began to understand the concept of holistic scoring. It made sense to give greater importance to the student's thinking—the processes they used to arrive at answers or to create products—than to the end results. However, I still found one important element missing for me. In the state of Texas, teachers are required by law to

give numerical grades to students. I needed a manageable way to use holistic scoring to arrive at my required numerical grades. This chapter explains the system I use to monitor my students' progress.

The system has two parts. First there are student responsibilities—records that they keep and commitments that they make, some of which are graded. Then there are teacher responsibilities: conferences with students, which enable me to keep track of their progress and give any necessary stimulus, and documentation or record-keeping.

Student Responsibilities

I use very few traditional worksheets in my Reading-Writing Workshop. Each student is involved in self-selected, not teacher-directed, reading and writing. So I use the following management techniques and open-ended forms that involve the students in documenting and assessing their work. These items have evolved from ideas gleaned here and there from workshops, books, and fellow teachers. I reshaped them to fit my particular needs. You will want to do the same.

STUDENT PORTFOLIO

This file folder contains samples of completed reading and writing projects. While the student shares the responsibility of deciding which samples of work to include in the portfolio, I accept responsibility for keeping the file. In addition to work samples, I also include other information (see page 41).

STUDENT FOLDERS

My students each have two folders with pockets. They label one Reading Folder and the other, Writing Folder. They keep all of their current work in these folders.

The Reading Folder has the student's Reading Log attached to one side with brads so it can easily be replaced as needed. The student keeps a Reading Contract in the pocket on the other side. If the student is working on a Reading Project, he or she also stores the plans in this pocket.

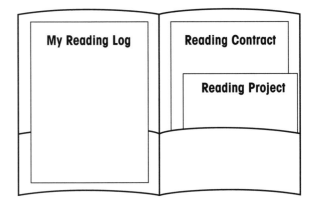

The Writing Folder has a copy of Brainstorms Worksheet attached to one side. This is where students keep an ongoing list of topics or ideas they may eventually want to write about. They use the other side of their writing folders to store their Journal and Peer Conference Diary. Students also keep plans for their Writing Projects here.

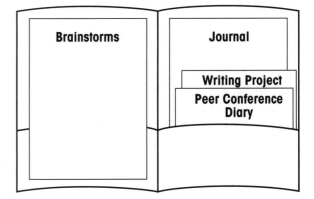

To understand how the folders help in evaluating student achievement, let's look at their contents in detail.

READING CONTRACT

This is the most important instrument in the Reading Folder. It provides a structured format for evaluating students' progress and assigning grades. It allows students to compete with themselves—not other students.

READING CONTRACT	
Name _____ Date _____	
These are the things I agree to do this week:	**Score**
1. I will read _____ books/pages.	_____
2. I will keep a daily reading log.	_____
3. I will summarize my reading.	_____
4. I will share my opinions about my reading.	_____
5. I will complete the skill assignment.	_____
Skill: _____ **Total**	_____
Comments: _____	

Each week I give my students a packet consisting of a Reading Contract (one-half page), four S.O.S. (Summary/ Opinion & Support) sheets (discussed below), and a page for skills assessment (worksheet or blank paper for recording). We staple these pages together and keep them in the Reading Folder in the student's desk.

Before I implemented my Reading-Writing Workshop, I based my students' reading grades primarily on their performance on worksheets. However, research such as that published in *Becoming a Nation of Readers: The Report of the Commission on Reading* indicates that the best way to improve reading skills is to spend more time reading, not more time on skills worksheets. I feel much more

comfortable with the grades derived from the Reading Contract. 40 percent of the students' grade is based on the quality of their independent reading time (1 and 2). Another 40 percent is based on how thoroughly they understand their self-selected reading (3 and 4). The last 20 percent is derived from their application of skills (5).

By the end of a week, students can accumulate up to 100 points on the contract. I use that score as the student's weekly reading grade. Because the contract grade represents a week's worth of work, it is weighted more heavily when I average final grades for the report card.

Students earn 0 to 20 points on each of these five contract responsibilities:

1. I will read _____ books/pages.

When my students pick up their contract packet on Monday, they set a reading goal. This goal reflects the amount of material they can read independently in 20 to 30 minutes. Each student sets his or her own goal. Advanced readers may decide how many pages or chapters they will read. Beginning readers may choose to read a certain number of books. Obviously, the student's reading ability and the difficulty of the books will be determining factors.

Daily goals are easier for younger students to comprehend. Older students may choose to set daily or weekly goals. The goals themselves do not affect the students' grades. They simply provide guides for determining how much and how long the students read independently each day.

Initially, my students had difficulty

setting realistic goals and needed more guidance. I planned a few minutes of class time at the end of each week to evaluate and discuss their reading goals. We talked about why they might have had trouble meeting their goals, and compared the merits of setting challenging goals that are not quite met to setting goals that are easily attained. I encouraged them to use this week's information to set more realistic goals for the next week.

The points I award for setting and meeting goals reflect the student's willingness to use the independent reading time wisely. For example, students who meet their goals by skimming through books without much comprehension will earn fewer points than those who absorb their books but fall short of their goal. Most students who are off-task during this time are uncomfortable selecting an appropriate book. So I help them find books on their reading level or in their topics of interest. Occasionally students continue this off-task behavior. I document this

on their Reading Log (see below) with a short note beside that day's reading entry. At the end of the week, I subtract points on this section of the contract.

2. I will keep a daily reading log.

My students must "log in" before they begin reading each day. My Reading Log is the record-keeping form on which they write the date, the author, the book title, and the page on which they begin reading. At the end of the independent reading time they "log out" by writing the number of the last page read. Some students will read more than one short book during this independent reading time. They will log each book in and out. Other students will take more than one day to read a longer book. They will log this same book in and out each day.

For young readers, you may need to modify the information required. For example, students can use a date stamp to record the date. Also, you might code a book with a number on the cover or library pocket. This way, students can record the book number instead of

Name	Michael

MY READING LOG
▼▼▼▼▼▼▼▼▼▼▼▼▼▼▼▼▼▼▼▼

Date	Author	Title	Pages
9-5	Lionni	Swimmy	1 - 7
9-6	Lionni	Swimmy	8 - 29
9-9	Kellogg	Best Friends *Sept 6. off task -2 pts.*	1 - 33
9-10	Mindrik	Little ○	1 - 19

Date	Author	Title		Pages
4-14-92	Steig	49		1-31
4-20-92	Lobel	81		1-27

Name Kimberly

MY READING LOG

writing the title and author.

Students earn up to four points a day for completing this information. Moreover, they begin to appreciate their own growth in reading. As this happens I hear comments like, "Look how many pages I read today!" and "This is the longest book I've ever read!"

3. I will summarize my reading.

4. I will share my opinions about my reading.

My students use their S.O.S. (Summary/ Opinion & Support) sheets to record these two contract responsibilities, for which they have a chance to earn one to five points each day on each responsibility. Although my students have independent reading every day, they do not complete an S.O.S. sheet on Friday, when I use this time for a skills assessment activity. If you have your students complete an S.O.S. sheet every day, each S.O.S. responsibility will count one to four points.

Students who read more than one book during the independent reading time will choose only one of the books to summarize. Students who read books that are too long to complete in one sitting will summarize the part they read that day. (Refer to chart at the top of page 30.)

Students use the lower half of the S.O.S. sheet for telling what they liked or disliked about their reading selection, and giving reasons to support their opinions. They color in all three stars if they think the book is excellent, two stars if they think it is average, and one star if they did not especially like it. (Refer to chart at bottom of page 30.)

When grading the S.O.S. sheets, I focus on what the students say, not on how they record their ideas. In other words, my main concern is their depth of understanding, not spelling, punctuation, or handwriting. I also allow for differences in reading level among my students. For example, one of my gifted second graders was reading Robert Louis Stevenson's *Treasure Island* while another student was reading Dr. Seuss's *Green Eggs and Ham*, yet I gave both of them the same score on their summaries and opinions.

It is easier for me to keep up with the scoring if I do it daily. As my students

Title Herbie Jones

Author Suzy Kline   **Pages Read** 1-20

Summary

This book is about a boy named Herbie and his friend Raymond. They try to get out of the lowest redding level. Herbie was the only one to get a 100 on his spelling test. Raymond tried to charm the teacher.

complete this task, I ask them to turn in the contract packets opened up to that day's S.O.S. sheet. Then I can score their responses without having to flip through the pages.

At first I found it helpful to read all of the day's S.O.S. sheets at once. This allowed me to become familiar with my class's ability range. Initially, I concentrated on either the summary response or the opinion response. It was easy to see the difference between the

responses of students who comprehended well and those who didn't.

As I read the S.O.S. sheets, I sorted the papers into three stacks: average, below average, and above average. Then I reread the above-average stack. If I still agreed with my first impression, I marked the summary or opinion with a check-plus. Next, I reread the average stack and marked these with a check. Finally, I reread the below-average stack,

OPINION AND SUPPORT

I thought it was exiting when Herbie's dad found a postcard saying Herbie got a 100 on his Spelling test because Herbie never got that before. My Mom looks for my 100!

Character	Funny Part	Illustrator
Sad Part	Free Choice	Setting
Exciting Part	Author	Surprising Part

marked these with a check-minus, and wrote a short comment or question that would help the student redirect his or her thinking and improve on the next try.

Whenever I make a comment, I require the students to initial it the next day when they get their contract packets. This ensures that they look for and read the comments. Below is a sample of my response to one student.

After a few days of this routine, you'll become quite confident and will be able to grade the entire S.O.S. sheet at your convenience and with the same ease you'd feel grading any fill-in-the-blank worksheet. Daily scoring is especially important at the beginning of the year when your students are still learning what you expect in a summary and an opinion.

As mentioned, my state mandates that numerical grades be given. Therefore I assign a score to each check-plus, check, or check-minus, then add those points to the other contract points in order to come up with a weekly numerical grade. A check-plus is worth five points, a check is worth four points, and a check-minus is worth between one and three points.

I send most checked S.O.S sheets home to the students' parents. Throughout the year I save a few sample S.O.S. sheets to document the growth in each student's ability to summarize and give supported opinions about reading selections. We file these in the Student Portfolio.

5. I will complete the skill.

Each week during my Skills lesson time I stress one or two main skills or strategies. The skill assignment evaluates how well my students can apply this skill.

Sometimes I use an appropriate worksheet from the basal series or the English textbook to evaluate them. Other times I use writing samples. For example, when my skill focus is on using content clues, I read a passage and then ask my students to write an explanation of several words in the passage. Sometimes the skill assignment may take the form of a learning center activity.

Whichever format I use, the students receive 0 to 20 points on the contract, depending on the degree of competency they demonstrate.

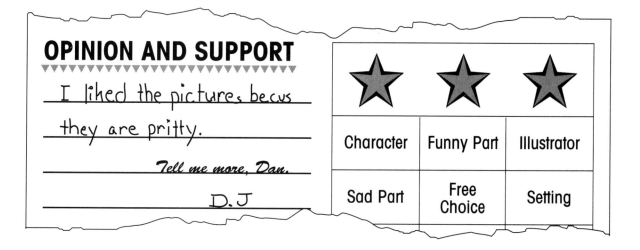

PEER CONFERENCE DIARY

The only one record-keeping item in the Writing Folder is the Peer Conference Diary. Students use this to summarize peer conferences about reading and writing projects. I reproduce the form shown on page 46, cut it apart, and assemble eight to ten pages in a small booklet (like the one below).

When a student completes a rough draft of a Writing Project or the plan of a Reading Project, it's time for a Peer Conference. The student meets with two other students to discuss the questions on the form. Afterward, the author returns to his or her seat to summarize the conference in the Peer Conference Diary. The questions on the form are designed to focus the student's attention on the structure and content of the Writing or Reading Project and on how well others understood his or her purpose. It helps the student rethink what he or she said and provides a direction for any necessary revisions.

Through peer conferences students are able to give and get help from each other that will improve their writing. Once we establish this spirit of community, my students begin to give and receive constructive suggestions with ease.

The ultimate goal of these peer conferences is to help students learn to rely less on me and more on their peers. Students often see the teacher's judgment as the only one that counts. I want to help them become independent, self-sufficient readers and writers capable of evaluating and forming their own opinions. Also, some students feel less intimidated discussing their work with other students.

I do not become involved in peer conference groups unless a problem arises. I establish appropriate rules of behavior, designate a specific area of the room for peer conferences, and set a limit on the number of groups allowed to meet at one time. Role-playing different situations has proven to be my most effective means of redirecting

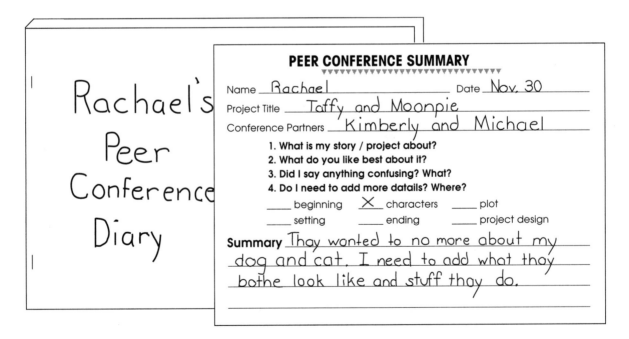

Rachael's
Peer
Conference
Diary

PEER CONFERENCE SUMMARY

Name __Rachael_____ Date __Nov. 30____
Project Title ___Taffy and Moonpie_____
Conference Partners ___Kimberly and Michael_____

1. What is my story / project about?
2. What do you like best about it?
3. Did I say anything confusing? What?
4. Do I need to add more details? Where?

____ beginning   _X_ characters   ____ plot
____ setting   ____ ending   ____ project design

Summary __They wanted to no more about my__
__dog and cat. I need to add what they__
__bothe look like and stuff they do.__

behavior. It is also helpful to keep reminding myself that cooperation is a long-range goal.

SAMPLE PEER CONFERENCE RULES

When you need a peer conference:

1. Choose 2 peers to meet with you.

2. Confer quietly.

3. Listen respectfully to all ideas.

4. Thank your peer partners.

5. Summarize and revise by yourself.

Teacher Responsibilities

The Reading-Writing Workshop provides a structure that maximizes the amount of quality time I have with my students. Therefore I've designed various strategies that enable me to both help students and evaluate their work without compromising the efficient use of my time. Here are the major strategies, together with the supporting documentation, I've found most effective. You can adapt these forms and charts to meet your own needs.

QUICK CHECK

After my students have had 30 to 45 minutes of Independent Work time, I have a Quick Check. I ring a bell twice (any other management technique for getting your students' attention will work) and say, "Quick Check." When I call out the students' names, they use a word or short phrase to tell me which tasks from the Flow Chart they are doing. For example, if I call on Stephen, who is writing a story about turtles, he might reply "rough draft."

I record this information on the Quick-Check Chart (See page 34). It takes me less than five minutes to complete a Quick Check of my 20 to 25 students once I have established the procedure and my students are familiar with the language of the Flow Chart. I keep the Quick-Check Chart on a clipboard, but you could post it on a bulletin board or clip it to your Lesson Plan. It provides a handy reference of students' progress throughout the week.

The Quick-Check Chart also directs my attention to students who are staying on one task too long. I can then arrange conferences if they need help, or set time limits if they have failed to use their time wisely. For example, I may say, "Chris, I see that you've been working on your rough draft for three days. Would you like to share it with me today or first thing tomorrow?" This gives the student a face-saving way out of a sticky situation. If he has been wasting time, he still has a class period to get finished. I make a shorthand note on the Quick-Check Chart to remind myself to ask for the rough draft.

Occasionally, I use a Quick Check as a management technique during Independent Work. If I find a large number of students off-task, I simply have another Quick Check to redirect their behavior. However, I've found that this technique loses its effectiveness if it is overused. I try to keep the

QUICK CHECK
▼▼▼▼▼▼▼▼▼▼▼▼▼▼

DAILY TASKS			WRITING PROJECT (W)			READING PROJECT (R)		
J	=	Journal	SM	=	Story Map	CB	=	Choose a Book
SQ	=	SQUIRT	RD	=	Rough Draft	R	=	Read
SOS	=	S.O.S.	C	=	Peer Conference	MP	=	Make a Plan
			RV	=	Revise	C	=	Peer Conference
			ED	=	Edit	RV	=	Revise
			L	=	Layout	ED	=	Edit
			PUB	=	Publish	PR	=	Project

Date

Name	10-15	10-16	10-17	10-18	10-19	10-21	10-22						
Erin	SM	RD	RD	C	RV	ED	L						
Cameron	SOS	RV	RV	ED	L	Pub	Pub						
Heather	CB	R	R	R	MP	C	RV						
John	C	RV	RV	ED	L	ED	RV						
Casey	SM	ED	RD	L	RV	RD	PC						
Melissa	SM	RD	L	C	ED	ED	L						

Independent Work period as free of interruptions as possible. We have all experienced frustration at having our work constantly interrupted, which usually results in a loss of both quality and motivation.

STUDENT-TEACHER CONFERENCES

During Independent Work I confer with individuals or with small groups of students who have a common need. I never leave these meetings to chance. While I allow time for the spontaneous conference needs that inevitably arise each day, I also have a plan for meeting with each student at least once a week for a Reading Conference and a Writing Conference.

WEEKLY CONFERENCE CHART

This chart (see page 35) helps organize the conferences. It was easiest for me to establish a consistent schedule for meeting with each child. For example, Kimberly's Reading Conference is every Monday and her Writing Conference is every Wednesday. However, you may want to post a new Conference Chart at the beginning of each week and let your students choose their Reading and Writing Conference times.

I attach the Weekly Conference Chart to my lesson plans for easy access.

If there is a specific need, I make a note of it beside the student's name. However, I begin most conferences by saying, "Tell me about your reading

Weekly Conference Schedule for the Week of _Jan. 24 - 28_

MONDAY

Reading	Writing
Michael – wants to try chapter book	_Kimberly_
Rachael	_Stephen – teach quotation marks_
Charlie	

(writing)." As the student talks about the book (or story), my teaching focuses on the needs that emerge from the conversation.

If the student seems unable to discuss the work, I know he or she is probably having difficulty comprehending the book or has no direction for writing. At that point, I ask the student to read favorite pages from the book (or read his or her writing). The conference focus becomes basic comprehension.

When the student is obviously right on target and there are no evident needs, I say, "It sounds like you're really enjoying this book. What kind of book do you want to try next?" or "It sounds like you know exactly what you want to say in this story. I'll look forward to reading it."

CONFERENCE SUMMARY SHEET

This is a valuable tool for documenting the skills I introduce, reteach, or enrich

Stephen Pillow

Date	Conference Summary
_9-2_	_Stephen is reading The Polar Express. Discussed similies in book: rolling over peaks and through valleys like a car on a roller coaster._
_9-9_	_Discussed how to use context clues to figure out meaning of new words._
_9-13_	_Wow! He used simile in camp out story._
_9-16_	_Topic—possessive nouns (Jim's dog). Reteach._

SKILLS MASTERY CHECKLIST

▼▼▼▼▼▼▼▼▼▼▼▼▼▼▼▼▼▼▼▼▼▼▼▼▼▼▼▼▼

Student _Stephen Pillow_	INTRODUCED	APPLIED	MASTERED	COMMENTS
COMPREHENSION				
Main Idea	X			_Sept. 6 – Introduced stated main idea_
Sequence of Events			X	_Nov. 30 – Successfully ordered and elaborated 5 actions in story_
Cause and Effect		X		_Feb. 16 – Used in his own writing: "The Boat Race"_
Drawing Conclusions	X			_Oct. 15 – Having difficulty identifying story clues_
Predicting Outcomes			X	_May 21 – Good support for predictions_
WORD ANALYSIS				
Basic Phonics Skills				

during the Reading and Writing Conferences. It clearly shows how I am meeting the individual needs of my students. A special form is not necessary. I use lined notebook paper to include the date and a summary of the conference. This ongoing page of notes is kept in each student's portfolio (see page 41).

My conference summaries are not detailed (see page 35); rather, they are brief notes regarding the nature of the conference. At the end of each conference, I say, "I want to make some notes about our conference. What would you like me to say that we talked about?" This brings closure to the conference and acts as a quick evaluation of the student's comprehension of our discussion.

If the student can't tell me what we discussed, that's a good indication that he or she did not grasp the concept. In

that case, I close by saying, "We discussed how to use quotation marks. I'm going to make myself a note that we want to review this again at our next conference."

I find that Conference Summary Notes are an excellent reference to use when conferring with parents. It helps them understand how I'm meeting their child's specific needs.

SKILLS MASTERY CHECKLIST

During my weekly reading and writing conferences, I use this checklist (see above) to record the new strategies or skills that I introduced. As a student begins to apply the skill, I record that. When a student has applied a skill consistently over a period of time, I mark it off as a mastered skill. I don't necessarily use this checklist at every conference—only when needed. I keep the checklist in the Student Portfolio.

Note that this is not intended to be a comprehensive list of reading and writing skills but simply the major skills needed by good readers and writers. I evaluate students according to the expectations of their grade level. Thus I would expect a third-grade student to recognize more difficult sight words than a first grader.

At first all this conferencing seems overwhelming! Here are a few suggestions that help make my conference time more productive and manageable.

READING CONFERENCE

The purpose of this conference is to assess and direct the student's reading. The Reading Conference may involve listening to the student read, teaching a specific reading strategy, or discussing a book.

You may want beginning readers to read aloud from a self-selected book. As the student reads, pay attention to the kinds of errors he or she makes. You can use these observations to plan future mini-lessons. Sometimes I use these lessons with one student during a Reading Conference time. Sometimes I teach them to a small group of students who all need the same strategy. When many students demonstrate a need for the mini-lesson, it becomes my class Skills lesson.

Sometimes I use Reading Conferences to discuss particular aspects of the books—such as character, mood, plot development, or the author's purpose in writing. Then the conferences become a time to stretch students' thinking and lead them to a deeper understanding of their books.

Most of my weekly Reading Conferences last from two to five minutes. You may feel that you need to meet with beginning readers more often than once a week. However, rather than trying to do too much as you begin implementing this Reading-Writing Workshop, adapt one of the following techniques to fit your schedule:

READ AROUND: As my students are involved in their independent reading, I rotate around the room. When I kneel beside a particular student, he or she begins to read aloud softly. When I stand up, the child continues reading silently. Typically, I stay just long enough to hear one page. A smile and a supportive pat are my only comments at this time. If a student seems to need help, I make a note to schedule an additional reading conference. I use a chart to keep track of which students I hear read each day.

READING TAPE: Individual students read one page of their choice on a tape. This requires some initial training time to teach students how to use the tape recorder, how to listen first to be sure they aren't recording over someone else's reading, and how to begin with their name, date, and the title of their book before reading. Five to ten students can record each day. I listen to the tape at my convenience and make notes about the kinds of errors students make.

WRITING CONFERENCE

Writing Conferences give my students an opportunity to meet with me at least once a week to discuss their writing. I try to keep these conferences between two and five minutes in length.

During a conference, I may discuss any particular problem the student has, such as difficulty with a writing skill. I may also discuss the evaluation of a completed Writing Project. In general, however, there are three kinds of Writing Conferences:

PREWRITING CONFERENCES: These are useful when students need help getting started. This "writer's block" happens most frequently when students try to write about unfamiliar plots or topics. When this happens, I try to redirect them to topics they know well; for example, what happened the first time they went bowling.

When students have difficulty writing about their own lives or simply want to try writing make-believe stories, I encourage them to use new characters with plots that they already know well. Instead of telling about a time a student felt lonely, he or she may write about a lonely mouse.

REVISING CONFERENCES: These occur after students have finished a piece of writing. They involve discussions about writing content (what was said) and not mechanics (punctuation, capitalization, spelling).

First, the student reads the piece of writing. I begin by giving honest, specific praise for some aspect of it. For example, "Your story's beginning really captured my interest" or "You really used some descriptive words."

Next, I ask questions that will help the student evaluate if the reader understands what was written. For example, "I was confused when you said. . . ," "What did you mean here?" or "How does this fit with the rest of your story?"

After the student explains what he or she meant, I simply ask, "How can you say that so the reader will understand what you mean?" or "Is there something you could add that would help the reader understand what you just told me?" Once the student understands, the conference is over, and he or she decides how best to make the revisions.

In a successful revising conference, the student does most of the talking. It is important to avoid making content suggestions! Once I begin telling a student how to make changes, the child loses ownership of the writing.

Sometimes I find myself trying to correct all of the student's writing problems through one piece of writing. This causes frustration both for the student and for me. Instead, I try to focus on one main problem. Students need praise and encouragement for each correct approximation. Each new story provides another opportunity to help the student become more proficient.

EDITING CONFERENCES: These focus on the mechanics of writing, including punctuation, capitalization, and spelling. We don't edit every piece of writing, but do make sure to edit those that will be published. Prior to introducing the writing process (Skills lesson 3, page 101), you will need to decide the best way to handle editing with your students.

It is possible to conduct all of the editing conferences yourself. However, my students become such serious, prolific writers that the task becomes overwhelming for one person. If at all possible, make use of volunteers.

I use parent volunteers to help with this task. Two or three volunteers come in one hour each week during Independent Work time to meet with students who have pieces of writing ready to edit. (My volunteers also type up the students' final drafts: see Skills lesson 9, page 120-123.) Usually each volunteer comes on a different day. At the beginning of the year, I conduct a brief training session with them to explain the purpose and procedure of this editing. This is the procedure my volunteers use:

1. Upon arriving they check the Edit box. This is where students put their revised writing when they are ready for editing help (see Writing Project Corner page 56).

2. Each volunteer takes one student into the hall. This allows the pairs to talk without distracting others.

3. The volunteer has a colored pencil for making editing marks. Students have the choice of marking the corrections themselves or having the volunteers act as their "secretaries."

4. The student reads the writing aloud. This helps avoid instances where the volunteer can't read the student's invented spellings. As the student reads, the volunteer makes corrections, stopping the student to briefly discuss each one. While it is not my volunteer's responsibility to teach these skills, this discussion helps involve the student in the editing and provides some corrective feedback.

5. The volunteer always confines his or her attention to editing the mechanical aspects of writing—not revising the content.

6. The student returns to class with the edited writing and puts it in a box labeled Publish. That gives me an opportunity to look over the papers before they are published and make notes about the major kinds of errors the students made. These become the topics of future Writing Conferences. The thoroughness with which we edit students' writing depends largely on their ability to edit for themselves and on how much final editing parent volunteers and I can realistically accomplish. It is most important to help students realize the *need* to use standard spelling and punctuation when their writing is being published for others to read.

Depending on your situation, it may be more realistic to allow students to publish when most but not all of their mistakes have been edited. If so, explain that their editing goal is to make their writing conform to standard spelling and punctuation as much as possible. However, because they are still learning, they will not always find every mistake. As they acquire more skills throughout the year, they should feel free to go back and correct mistakes they have missed.

Editing is one of the least glamorous steps in the writing process. As you decide how to handle it, keep in mind your larger goal of developing not only proficient but also enthusiastic writers. The more your students write, the better they will write. Establish an editing plan that fosters their love for writing as they continue developing their skills.

READING PROJECT CONFERENCE

For the most part, students complete their Reading Projects without my assistance. Once in a while, however, a student will need to meet to clarify an idea.

WRITING EVALUATION

You will need to decide whether or not you want your students to publish everything they write. You may make this decision the writer's responsibility, leaving each student free to decide which, if any, writing will be published. Or you may establish guidelines, but allow the students to choose what they will do to satisfy your requirements. In either case, rough drafts that students choose not to publish might be filed in a portfolio or writing folder where students could return to them at a later date, or you may decide to send the drafts home marked "Rough Copy" or "Unedited."

I do not grade most of my students' writing. Instead, I use conferences to informally evaluate and teach writing skills. However, periodically I ask my students to choose their best piece of writing to be graded. Sometimes I may specify the type of writing. Following a study of descriptive writing, for example, I may request that my students give me a story with their best description in it. If I'm stressing catchy topic sentences, I may ask students to turn in writing with a beginning that grabs the reader's attention. Occasionally, the whole grade is based on the evaluation of this specific part of the story.

THE WRITING INVENTORY

The Writing Inventory is designed to provide a standard yet flexible tool for evaluating the selected writing. Students can earn up to 34 points for their performance in each of three categories. Alternatively, you can evaluate each category by using a check for average, a check-plus for above average, and a check-minus for below average. The Writing Inventory Matrix on page 42 outlines expectations for each category. The three categories for good writing are:

STRUCTURE: Good writing has a beginning, middle, and end. It has a topic sentence that lets the reader know the purpose of the writing. The middle, or main body of writing, has an organized, sequenced structure. It ends with a closing sentence that lets the reader know the piece is finished. This may be written as a summary, a concluding opinion, or a "happily ever after" statement that briefly tells what happened after the story's problem was resolved.

ELABORATION: This refers to the way an author develops and supports the main ideas with appropriate details. The difference between a mediocre piece of writing and one that holds the reader's attention is elaboration. A number of techniques may be use to elaborate:

▶ *Varied and complex sentence patterns*

▶ *Descriptive adjectives*

▶ *Dialogue or quotations*

▶ *Similes, metaphors, and hyperboles*

▶ *Detailed descriptions of characters, setting, and feelings*

MECHANICS: The score here reflects how well the student uses age-appropriate spelling, basic sentence structures, capitalization, and punctuation. I also evaluate noun/verb agreement and the use of pronouns. If handwriting is so poor that the work is illegible, then I deduct points from this category.

Two Writing Inventory forms are reproduced. The second one (page 53) is a simplified version that students can use for self-evaluation. However, older students can be taught to use the regular Writing Inventory form (page 52) to evaluate their own writing. One fifth-grade teacher records her evaluation in the "Second Opinion" column and has the students complete the "My Opinion" column. She feels that this sends a subtle message to the students that their opinions are as valuable as her own. In fact, she finds most of her students are much more critical of their own writing than she is. She averages the student's writing evaluation in with her own. For example, if the student arrives at a total score of 86, while her score is 90, she uses the average, 88.

READING PROJECT EVALUATION

Only rarely do I make a formal evaluation of a student's reading project. I then use the form reproduced on pages 50 and 51. You may wish to simplify or modify this for your own use.

STUDENT PORTFOLIO

I have mentioned this several times in the course of this chapter, but now is the time to review all of its contents together.

Each student's portfolio contains:

▶ *The student's selection of Reading Projects*

▶ *The student's selection of Writing Projects*

▶ *Completed sheets of My Reading Log (a record of what the student has read)*

▶ *Your selection of Summary/Opinion & Support Sheets (a record of how well the student has read)*

▶ *Conference Summary Sheets (a record of problems, skills, etc., that you have discussed with the student)*

▶ *Skills Mastery Checklist (a record of proficiency in reading and writing skills)*

By consulting the portfolio you can very easily refresh your memory about the student's past progress and present stage of development, and thus decide what help he or she may need for future improvement.

WRITING INVENTORY MATRIX

	✓+ (30–34 Points)	✓ (26–29 Points)	✓– (22–25 Points)
S T R U C T U R E	• Beginning – clearly communicates purpose or story problem • Middle – sequenced • End – resolves problem and includes resolution statement (happily-ever-after)	• Beginning – purpose or story problem is understandable • Middle – sequenced, but action may not flow smoothly from event to event • End – a conclusion is attempted, but it may not resolve the problem • No resolution statement (happily-ever-after)	• Rambles or changes focus • Beginning – no clear purpose or introduction of characters or setting • Middle – confusing organization • End – no conclusion
E L A B O R A T I O N	• Main ideas are fully developed and supported with details • Interesting and varied sentence patterns • Specific words used (*glamorous* rather than *pretty*) • Uses adjectives, adverbs, quotations, similes, and metaphors to describe	• Main ideas developed, but not fully supported with details • Some varied sentence patterns • Some specific words • Some use of adjectives, adverbs, and/or quotations to describe	• Main ideas not fully developed • Little supporting detail • Same basic sentence pattern repeated throughout writing • Many sentences begin with *and* or other connectors • No specific words used
M E C H A N I C S	• Few capitalization or punctuation errors • Grade-appropriate words spelled correctly • Uses correct noun/verb agreement • Pronouns used effectively	• Some capitalization and punctuation errors • Uses functional spelling throughout the writing – does not affect its readability • Some errors in noun/verb agreement	• Spelling, punctuation, and capitalization errors make writing difficult to read • Many incomplete or run-on sentences • Illegible handwriting

READING CONTRACT

▼▼▼▼▼▼▼▼▼▼▼▼▼▼▼▼▼▼

Name _____ Date _____

These are the things I agree to do this week: **Score**

    1. I will read _____ books/pages.   _____

    2. I will keep a daily reading log.   _____

    3. I will summarize my reading.   _____

    4. I will share my opinions about my reading.   _____

    5. I will complete the skill assignment.   _____

        Skill: _____   **Total** _____

Comments: _____

_____

_____

READING CONTRACT

▼▼▼▼▼▼▼▼▼▼▼▼▼▼▼▼▼▼

Name _____ Date _____

These are the things I agree to do this week: **Score**

    1. I will read _____ books/pages.   _____

    2. I will keep a daily reading log.   _____

    3. I will summarize my reading.   _____

    4. I will share my opinions about my reading.   _____

    5. I will complete the skill assignment.   _____

        Skill: _____   **Total** _____

Comments: _____

_____

_____

Name _____

MY READING LOG

Date	Author	Title	Pages

Name _____ Date _____

S.O.S.
▼▼▼▼▼▼▼▼▼ ▼▼

Title _____

Author _____ Pages Read _____

Summary

_____

_____

_____

_____

_____

_____

- -

OPINION AND SUPPORT
▼▼▼▼▼▼▼▼▼▼▼▼▼▼▼▼▼▼▼▼▼▼▼▼▼▼▼

_____

_____

_____

_____

_____

☆	☆	☆
Character	Funny Part	Illustrator
Sad Part	Free Choice	Setting
Exciting Part	Author	Surprising Part

_____

_____

_____

_____

PEER CONFERENCE SUMMARY
▼▼▼▼▼▼▼▼▼▼▼▼▼▼▼▼▼▼▼▼▼▼▼▼▼▼▼▼▼

Name _____ Date _____

Project Title _____

Conference Partners _____

    1. What is my story / project about?
    2. What do you like best about it?
    3. Did I say anything confusing? What?
    4. Do I need to add more details? Where?

    _____ beginning   _____ characters   _____ plot
    _____ setting   _____ ending   _____ project design

Summary _____

_____

_____

_____

- -

PEER CONFERENCE SUMMARY
▼▼▼▼▼▼▼▼▼▼▼▼▼▼▼▼▼▼▼▼▼▼▼▼▼▼▼▼▼

Name _____ Date _____

Project Title _____

Conference Partners _____

    1. What is my story / project about?
    2. What do you like best about it?
    3. Did I say anything confusing? What?
    4. Do I need to add more details? Where?

    _____ beginning   _____ characters   _____ plot
    _____ setting   _____ ending   _____ project design

Summary _____

_____

_____

_____

QUICK CHECK

▼▼▼▼▼▼▼▼▼▼▼▼▼▼▼

DAILY TASKS			WRITING PROJECT (W)			READING PROJECT (R)		
J	=	Journal	SM	=	Story Map	CB	=	Choose a Book
SQ	=	SQUIRT	RD	=	Rough Draft	R	=	Read
SOS	=	S.O.S.	C	=	Peer Conference	MP	=	Make a Plan
			RV	=	Revise	C	=	Peer Conference
			ED	=	Edit	RV	=	Revise
			L	=	Layout	ED	=	Edit
			PUB	=	Publish	PR	=	Project

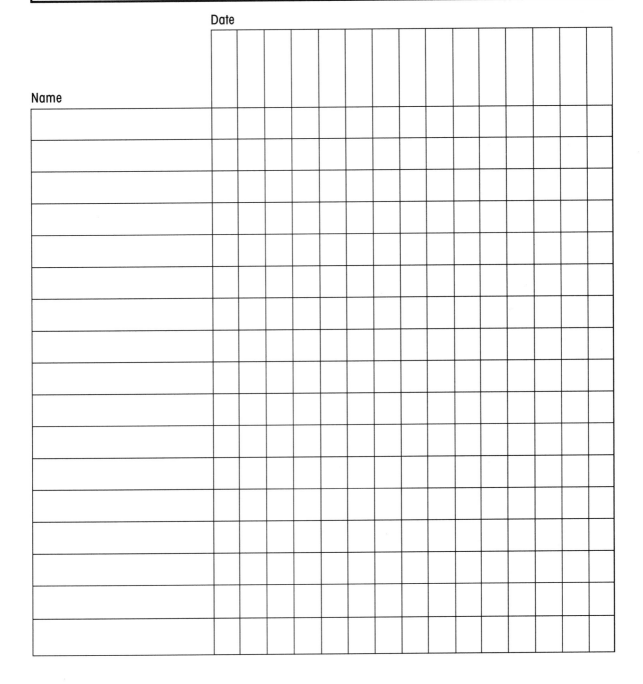

Date

Name

Weekly Conference Schedule for the Week of _____

MONDAY
Reading   **Writing**

_____
_____
_____
_____
_____

TUESDAY
Reading   **Writing**

_____
_____
_____
_____
_____

WEDNESDAY
Reading   **Writing**

_____
_____
_____
_____
_____

THURSDAY
Reading   **Writing**

_____
_____
_____
_____
_____

FRIDAY
Reading   **Writing**

_____
_____
_____
_____
_____

SKILLS MASTERY CHECKLIST

Student _____ COMPREHENSION	INTRODUCED	APPLIED	MASTERED	COMMENTS
Main Idea				
Sequence of Events				
Cause and Effect				
Drawing Conclusions				
Predicting Outcomes				
WORD ANALYSIS				
Basic Phonics Skills				
Sight Words				
Context Clues				
WRITING CONTENT				
Sequenced Beginning, Middle, End				
Supporting Details for Main Ideas				
Writing Styles: Descriptive				
Narrative				
Informative				
Compare/Contrast				
Persuasive				
WRITING MECHANICS				
Complete Sentences				
Noun/Verb/Pronoun Agreement				
Capital Letters (Beg. Sentence, Names, I)				
Periods, Question Marks, Exclamations				
Commas: Date, Address, Letter, Series				
Legible Handwriting				

READING PROJECT EVALUATION

▼▼▼▼▼▼▼▼▼▼▼▼▼▼▼▼▼▼▼▼▼▼▼▼▼▼▼▼▼▼▼▼▼▼▼▼▼▼

Name _____ Date _____

Project _____

Goal _____

The following rating scale is based on performance expectations for most second graders.

> 1 – Unsatisfactory
> 2 – Below expectations
> 3 – Meets expectations
> 4 – Exceeds expectations
> 5 – Clearly outstanding

1. **Development.** The project follows a logical order and has enough information to clearly present the ideas. It has an appropriate beginning and ending.

    1   2   3   4   5

2. **Sentence Structure.** Ideas are presented in complete sentences. The appropriate use of adverbs, adjectives, prepositions, and multiple ideas in a sentence shows advanced thinking and writing for a second grader.

    1   2   3   4   5

3. **Punctuation.** Capital letters and ending punctuation have been used appropriately.

    1   2   3   4   5

4. **Spelling.** Words appropriate for second graders have been spelled correctly.

    1   2   3   4   5

5. **Vocabulary.** Words were used correctly to convey meaning. A variety of words were used.

    1   2   3   4   5

6. **Visual Aids.** All visual aids are appropriate. They are neat and show sufficient detail to completely express the idea.

    1   2   3   4   5

7. **Following Directions.** Specific directions for this assignment were followed.

    1   2   3   4   5

8. **Research.** The project shows evidence of research and/or knowledge of the subject matter.

    1   2   3   4   5

9. **General Appearance.** The project is neat and complete.

    1   2   3   4   5

10. **Creativity.** The project reflects unique or inventive thinking.

    1   2   3   4   5

Score: 20–29 points = 73–79 percent
30–39 points = 80–89 percent
40–50 points = 90–100 percent

Grade:_____

Teacher Comments:_____

_____

_____

_____

• •

Date received_____ Date due_____

You may earn 5 to 10 bonus points by completing this section of the evaluation and returning it to me within 3 days. Discuss your ideas with your parents. They may record your ideas on this form for you.

1. List 3 ideas you have for improving your work on this project.

_____

_____

_____

2. List 3 things you did very well on this project. Tell why you think it is good work.

_____

_____

_____

3. What did you learn most from this assignment? How will this help you in the future?

_____

_____

_____

_____   _____
Student's signature   Parent's signature

WRITING INVENTORY

▼▼▼▼▼▼▼▼▼▼▼▼▼▼▼▼▼▼▼▼▼▼▼▼▼

Name _____ Date _____

Title _____

Score

| My Opinion | Second Opinion |

Structure (0–33 points)

_____ My writing has a beginning.

_____ My writing has a middle.

_____ My writing has an end.

_____   _____

Elaboration (0–34 points)

_____ My writing has details that tell about the main ideas.

_____ My writing uses interesting, descriptive words.

_____ My writing has different sentence patterns.

_____   _____

Mechanics (0–33 points)

_____ My writing uses nouns, verbs, and pronouns correctly.

_____ My writing has grade-level words spelled correctly.

_____ My writing uses capital letters and punctuation as needed.

_____   _____

Total [ ]   [ ]

Comments _____

_____

_____

_____

WRITING INVENTORY

Name_____ Date_____

Author _____

Title_____

Structure (0–33 points)

_____ My writing has a beginning.

_____ My writing has a middle.

_____ My writing has an end.

Elaboration (0–34 points)

_____ My writing has details that tell about the main ideas.

_____ My writing uses interesting, descriptive words.

_____ My writing has different sentence patterns.

Mechanics (0–33 points)

_____ My writing uses nouns, verbs, and pronouns correctly.

_____ My writing has grade-level words spelled correctly.

_____ My writing uses capital letters and punctuation as needed.

_____   _____
Student's signature   Teacher's signature

Comments _____

_____

_____

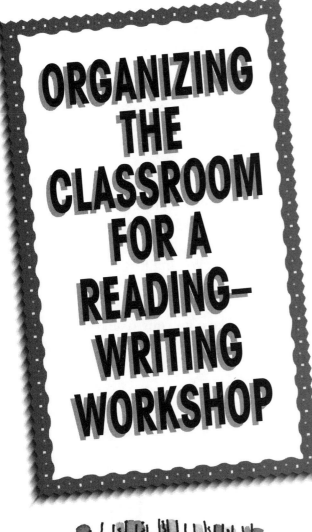

CHAPTER FOUR

ORGANIZING THE CLASSROOM FOR A READING-WRITING WORKSHOP

My classroom arrangement is limited by the amount of space I have— or more accurately, the space I *don't* have. Obviously, the more space you have to separate the different activities that will be occurring in your classroom, the better. Here are the special areas I need for my Reading-Writing Workshop and some techniques I use for making the most of my limited space.

CLASS LIBRARY

This is the primary source of books for my students during their independent reading time. Children's book clubs are an excellent resource. They offer quality literature at discount rates. Most of them give bonus points for each dollar spent, and you can use the points to purchase more books.

I have limited bookshelf space, so I keep books in plastic dishpans along a wall. Try these even if you have plenty of bookcase space. Because they provide easy access, students can quickly flip through the books and see the covers. Often an inviting cover will tempt a student to pick up the book and take a closer look.

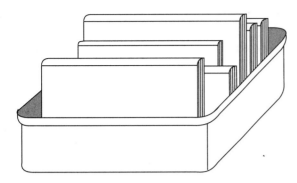

BORROWED BOOK NOOK

This is where I display the books that are on loan to my class from the local library, the school library, or my students' home libraries.

It was necessary for me to establish special rules for handling these borrowed books:

> **1.** Treat borrowed books as if they were your own.
>
> **2.** Borrowed books must stay in the classroom.
>
> **3.** Return borrowed books at the end of each day.

READING-WRITING CENTER

This is an area that I designate as a quiet zone. Students in this area are reading or writing independently, so talking stays at a minimum. In my classroom, the students' desk space is the quiet work area. Because my classroom is small and students must conduct peer conferences fairly close to this reading-writing center, I make headphones available to students who have difficulty screening out noise.

PEER CONFERENCE CORNER

This is a designated place where my students go to meet with one or two peers to discuss their Writing or Reading Projects. At one point, I allowed peer conference groups to meet in the hallway. However, this restricted my supervision of the groups and many students could not handle the additional freedom. Despite my efforts to keep the conferences quiet, I have learned to expect some noise from these areas of the room. Limiting my class to no more than three peer conference groups at one time seems to be effective in my small classroom.

WRITING PROJECT CORNER

After students have completed their peer conferences and made revisions, they take their Writing Projects to this area. I use five plastic tubs or dishpans called Journey Boxes, since the Writing Projects make a journey from tub to tub as they go through the final stages. My boxes are labeled this way:

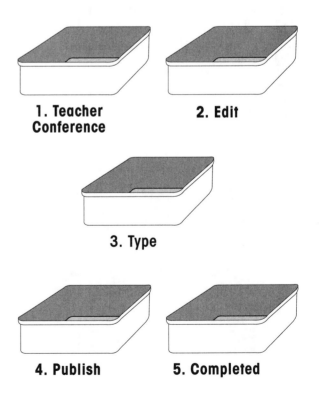

1. Teacher Conference   **2. Edit**

3. Type

4. Publish   **5. Completed**

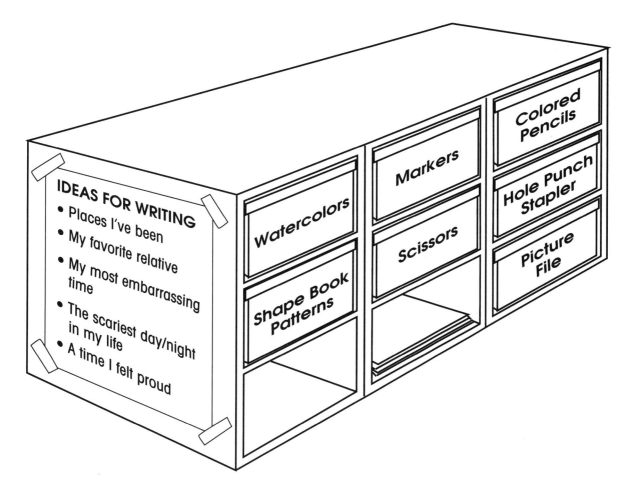

The Type Box is necessary only if you have volunteers who use a typewriter or word processor to transcribe the students' handwritten drafts.

PUBLISHING AREA

This is a corner, shelf, or table for storing the materials needed for bookmaking. I include writing paper (plain and fancy), construction paper for covers, colored pencils, markers, a stapler, a hole punch, a picture idea box (a collection of stimulating pictures), a topic idea box or poster (a general list of topics such as my best friend, most embarrassing moment, favorite relative, etc.), and tagboard patterns for making shape books. I've found that a nine-box shoe organizer is an efficient way to store these supplies.

AUTHORS' CORNER

This is a special corner for displaying students' writing. In my classroom it is an inexpensive lingerie drying rack suspended from the ceiling. Students hang their books for everyone to see. Your Authors' Corner might be an assigned shelf on a bookcase, a special tub, or a clothesline. Whatever you use, be sure that the students' writing is easily accessible. These books are by far the most popular in my classroom!

These are the basic work areas in my Reading-Writing Workshop. You will want to modify them and add your own creative touches to fit your students' needs.

CHAPTER FIVE

READING– WRITING WORKSHOP LESSONS

The lessons presented in this chapter are designed to help you implement a Reading-Writing Workshop in your classroom one step at a time. They have been used successfully with both upper and lower elementary students.

At first you will need to spend time teaching procedures and strategies. The Reading-Writing Workshop tasks are built on this foundation, and your students cannot undertake Independent Work without it. The stronger you make that foundation through modeling, role-playing, and carefully guided practice, the more self-reliant your students will become and the more smoothly your workshop will flow.

This chapter presents ten lessons each from the Literature Focus and Skills components. The selection includes all of the basic lessons needed to prepare your students for Independent Work and get your Reading-Writing Workshop fully under way. Initially, you'll start by using your Literature Focus time to teach the procedures and skills that students need in order to complete their Reading

Contract responsibilities, and your Skills time will be used to teach the writing process steps. Once you have accomplished those goals, you'll use your Literature Focus and Skills time to refine and present more sophisticated reading and writing strategies. Literature Focus lessons 7 through 10 provide specific examples (see Reading Projects below).

The lessons in each category are designed to be taught in sequence. For example, you'll want to teach Literature Focus lesson 4, and make sure your students thoroughly understand it, before you present the strategies in Literature Focus lesson 5. However, there's no reason why you can't use Skills lesson 6 and still be on Literature Focus lesson 4. It all depends on how well your students grasp the concepts presented in each category.

Each lesson has an easy-to-read structure. In addition to a lesson outline, you'll find background information, a time frame for teaching the concept, suggestions for literature to use, and extension activities. Each lesson introduces students to a particular task or strategy. Students will master some of these tasks quickly. Others involve higher levels of thinking and will require much more practice before students are ready to do them independently. Use the introductory lessons provided in this chapter as models when planning the follow-up lessons your students may need. Try repeating the same lesson using a different literature focus. The time frame suggested for presenting each concept is a guide only. As a general rule, you'll model a procedure first, then guide students through a controlled practice session. Finally, you'll give an assignment for students to attempt with minimal assistance from you. Students may need one lesson or many lessons to complete these steps.

Use the Implementation Overview on page 64 in planning and sequencing your daily lesson plans. Use the suggestions in each lesson guide to help develop additional reteaching or extension lessons.

Reading Projects

The last four Literature Focus lessons provide students with models of the kind of approach they may wish to choose for an independent Reading Project. Once they are familiar with these models, they can apply them to books of their own choice.

For an independent Reading Project, students first choose a book—probably one they read during SQUIRT (Sustained Quiet Uninterrupted Independent Reading Time). Then they reread the book. Next, they make a plan for sharing the book with the class. For younger students this may be a mental process, but they may also make sketches to show their plan. Older students will be able to write about their ideas. The project may involve relating the plot, describing characters, or investigating the author's or illustrator's style. For example, one student read several Leo Lionni books and then made a collage of his own to demonstrate Lionni's distinctive style of art.

After a student has a reading project plan, he or she follows the steps shown in the Flow Chart (page 18).

Ideas for Further Lessons

To develop further lessons, here are some strategies you might want to try. Since Skills lesson topics will arise mainly out of your students' needs and state or district requirements, these ideas emphasize Literature Focus strategies. However, I briefly indicate some Skills topics that you might conveniently spin off from the Literature Focus suggestions.

AUTHOR STUDIES

Studying an author or illustrator is a great way to introduce students to the concept of literature themes. For example, after reading Leo Lionni's *Alexander and the Wind-Up Mouse*, *Frederick*, and *Fish Is Fish*, my students were easily able to identify themes of pride and cooperation. From there, they read other books by Lionni, as well as other authors, to find additional stories that address these same themes.

LITERATURE THEMES

Grouping books by general literature themes is another approach to Literature Focus. We usually start with a broad theme and discuss the characteristics of books with this theme. For example, one third-grade class in my building explored *journeys*. They defined journey books as those in which characters take a significant journey, making the journey an integral part of the plot. After the teacher read aloud *The Polar Express* by Chris Van Allsburg, she discussed how the book fits the theme. Then, her class began a chart of journey books. After exploring several more examples as a class, the students brought in books of their own and supported the claim that these, too, were journey books.

JOURNEY BOOKS
▼▼▼▼▼▼▼▼▼▼▼▼▼

The Polar Express

Lon Po Po

The Three Little Pigs

Mike Mulligan and His Steam Shovel

Cinderella

Snow White

Treasure Island

Little Red Riding Hood

This might lead to a Skills lesson on verbs of motion.

CURRICULUM-BASED THEMES

In our school, a fifth-grade patriotism unit resulted in a Literature Focus on historical fiction. The teacher began by creating a time line with important historical events highlighted. Students read historical fiction and then placed their books on the time line. Literature helped recreate each time period and made it come alive for the students. It also helped the students recognize the difference between fact and fiction (see example on page 62).

This might lead to a Skills lesson on simple aspects of time (adverbs and adverbial phrases) and/or tense.

Likewise, my second-grade science unit on animals initiated a fact and fantasy study. My students read fiction

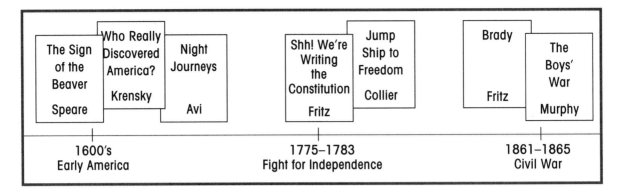

| The Sign of the Beaver — Speare | Who Really Discovered America? Krensky | Night Journeys Avi | Shh! We're Writing the Constitution Fritz | Jump Ship to Freedom Collier | Brady Fritz | The Boys' War Murphy |

1600's
Early America

1775–1783
Fight for Independence

1861–1865
Civil War

stories with animals as main characters. Then we made a chart comparing the character traits based on fact and those based on fantasy. This particular table could lead to a Skills lesson on the use of negatives.

MAKE WAY FOR DUCKLINGS
▼▼▼▼▼▼▼▼▼▼▼▼▼▼▼▼▼▼▼▼▼▼▼▼

by Robert McCloskey

FACT

Ducks fly

Foxes do hunt ducks

Ducks build nests near water

Ducks do molt

Ducks hatch from eggs

People might feed ducks peanuts

FICTION

Ducks do not talk

Ducks cannot count

Ducks do not name their babies

Policemen would not come to help ducks cross roads

Supporting Materials

What materials are required for Literature Focus? That depends on whether the particular objective lends itself to whole-class instruction or is better explored individually or in small groups.

Sometimes all of my students explore the same theme, but each one uses a different book. Other times I have my students investigate themes in small groups. For this grouping, I need sets of three to five copies of a title. Each group reads a different title.

I take advantage of quality paperback literature available from children's book clubs to build my collection of books relatively quickly and inexpensively. Several of the children's book clubs make this task even easier by classifying their literature according to broad themes such as friendship, responsibility, ecology, etc.

Literature Focus Materials

As a further resource, I make use of books borrowed from the local library, the school library, or my students' home libraries. Often I ask my students to share their own books on a particular topic with the class. Involving students in collecting these books has several benefits. It reduces my leg work and it

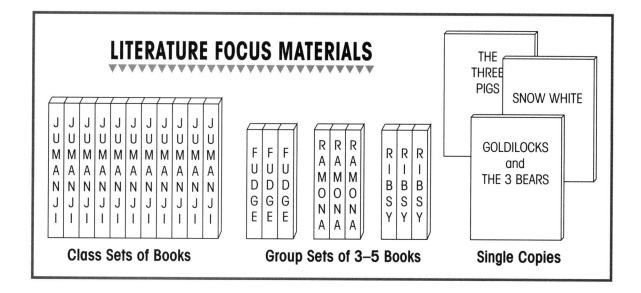

LITERATURE FOCUS MATERIALS

Class Sets of Books · Group Sets of 3–5 Books · Single Copies

increases the number of books I have available for my class. It also motivates students to do additional reading outside of class. As students hunt for books on a specific topic or theme, they must read, identify the main ideas, and categorize the books.

Borrowed books are particularly useful for integrating curriculum subjects. For example, if I'm teaching about the Civil War in social studies, I might make a collection of books on this topic available for my students to read during Independent Work. These could be both fiction and nonfiction books that I've borrowed from our school or local library.

The following books are excellent sources of ideas for Literature Focus and Skills lessons. The strategies the authors present are applicable to students of all ages.

Bringing It All Together
Terry D. Johnson and Daphne R. Louis (Heinemann, 1990)

Literacy Through Literature
Terry D. Johnson and Daphne R. Louis (Heinemann, 1987)

Teaching with Caldecott Books: Activities Across the Curriculum
Christine Boardman Moen (Scholastic, 1991)

As you begin building your own Reading-Writing Workshop, the most important ingredient will be a supportive, encouraging atmosphere that facilitates the development of competent, self-motivated, independent readers, writers, and thinkers. The time you invest in teaching and practicing the strategies in the following lessons will help you reach that goal efficiently and effectively.

IMPLEMENTATION OVERVIEW

LITERATURE FOCUS GOALS

Goal 1: **Choosing Books**
Time Frame: 1–2 days

Goal 2: **Independent Reading**
Time Frame: 1–2 days

Goal 3: **Summarize**
Time Frame: 5–10 days

Goal 4: **Identify Fact and Opinion**
Time Frame: 1–3 days

Goal 5: **Supporting Opinions**
Time Frame: 1–3 days

Goal 6: **Reading Contract**
Time Frame: 1 day

Goal 7–10 are optional reading projects.

Goal 7: **Reading Project: Can Do!**
Time Frame: 2–5 days

Goal 8: **Reading Project: Peek Overs**
Time Frame: 2–5 days

Goal 9: **Reading Project: Point of View**
Time Frame: 2–5 days

Goal 10: **Reading Project: Game Boards**
Time Frame: 2–5

SKILLS LESSON GOALS

Goal 1: **Writer's Journal**
Time Frame: 1–2 days

Goal 2: **Writing Topics**
Time Frame: 1 day

Goal 3: **Writing Process**
Time Frame: 1–2 days

Goal 4: **Story Mapping**
Time Frame: 1–2 days

Goal 5: **Story Beginnings**
Time Frame: 1–2 days

Goal 6: **Rough Draft**
Time Frame 1–2 days

Goal 7: **Conclusions**
Time Frame: 1–2 days

Goal 8: **Peer Conference**
Time Frame: 2–5 days

Goal 9: **Edit**
Time Frame: 1–3 days

Goal 10: **Publish**
Time Frame: 1–3 days

Future Skills Lessons can be used to teach any reading or writing skill (see page 17).

Getting Started:
LITERATURE FOCUS LESSONS

Choosing Books

OBJECTIVE

Students will learn strategies for choosing appropriate books to read independently.

TIME FRAME: 1–2 days

ADVANCE PREPARATIONS

1. Gather a selection of high-interest literature to read aloud.

2. Display four to five different types of books (riddles, fairy tales, poetry, etc.) along the ledge of the chalkboard.

3. Put six to eight books in a paper bag. Include a variety of different types. Prepare one bag for every group of three to five students.

BACKGROUND

Many students, even older ones, do not know how to choose books to read independently. They must develop strategies that will help them choose books on their reading and interest levels. They also need to be given permission to stop reading books they find too difficult or are not enjoying.

LITERATURE SUGGESTIONS

Any high-interest literature appropriate for your students' age level will work for this lesson.

Lesson Outline

GUIDANCE

Read your literature selection aloud. Explain that there are many different kinds of books—mysteries, fairy tales, animal stories, biographies, etc. Classify the literature selection you read aloud.

Direct students to think about what makes them want to read certain books. It may be the cover, the subject, or a recommendation from a friend. Then discuss reasons why they may not want to read a book. Remind students that it is a wise decision to return books that are too difficult or are uninteresting.

PRACTICE

1. Introduce the 5 Finger Rule. Ask students to read a page of their books and put up one finger for each word they do not know and cannot figure out.

If they find five unknown words on that page, they should probably choose another book. Next, as they continue reading, have them put up one finger for each page they read. They will usually become interested in a book in the first five pages of text. After reading five pages, they may choose to keep the book or put it back and choose another.

2. Give each group of four students a bag containing assorted books and have each group member choose a book to read. Allow about five minutes for group members to share their reasons for choosing particular books. Next ask them to use the 5 Finger Rule to help decide if they can read their books independently. If so, they will keep the books to read during Literature Focus lesson 2. If not, they will choose other books.

EXTENSION ACTIVITY

Make a bookmark to remind students of the 5 Finger Rule.

1. Fold a 9-by-6 inch piece of colored construction paper in half.

2. Place a hand on the paper with the edge of the palm on the fold. With fingers closed, trace one hand on the paper.

3. Cut out the hand shape. Be sure to cut through both layers of paper.

4. Draw lines to make fingers on the outside of each hand. Students write their names on the palm and different kinds of books they like to read on each finger.

5. Show students how to slip the hand over a page to hold their place in the book. Use the bookmark as a reminder of the 5 Finger Rule for choosing a book.

Independent Reading

OBJECTIVE
Students will be able to follow procedures for reading and recording their SQUIRT (Sustained Quiet Uninterrupted Independent Reading Time) books.

TIME FRAME: 1–2 days

ADVANCE PREPARATIONS

1. Each student needs a pocket folder. They will use this to prepare their Reading Folder (see page 26).

2. Reproduce a copy of My Reading Log (page 44) for each student.

3. Plan the specific rules you will enforce during SQUIRT.
For example: Remain quiet.
                Stay seated. Read!

BACKGROUND
Students should get into the habit of selecting their reading material before SQUIRT begins. This will allow them to focus their time on reading a book, not choosing a book.

You will need to intervene if a student consistently spends more time choosing books than reading them, or frequently returns unread books. Reluctant readers often use this delaying tactic. You may need to select three or four appropriate books for each of those students and let them choose one each to read.

LITERATURE SUGGESTIONS
Student-selected literature.

Lesson Outline

GUIDANCE
Ask students to pretend that someone gives them ten minutes to spend $1,000 in a toy store. At the end of ten minutes they have to return any money they have not spent. Will they use the time trying to decide what they want or buying toys?

Likewise, students will gain most from independent reading if they spend their time reading, not choosing books.

Direct your students' attention to the Log In, SQUIRT, and Log Out signs on the Flow Chart. Explain and model each task.

LOG IN

Before reading, students must record the date, title, and author of the chosen book, and the number of the first page they will be reading. Some picture books are not numbered. Discuss what to do in that case. (For example, they might use one for the first story page and count pages from there.)

SQUIRT

Explain that this stands for Sustained Quiet Uninterrupted Independent Reading Time. Discuss your rules for SQUIRT.

LOG OUT

Students record the number of the last page they read.

Stress the importance of logging in before beginning SQUIRT. Then, if a student's independent reading time is interrupted for any reason, he or she can quickly record the last page read. This will prevent unnecessary delays when you are ready to begin a whole class lesson.

Help students label and prepare their reading folders. Give each child a copy of My Reading Log. Use brads to fasten it to the Reading Folder.

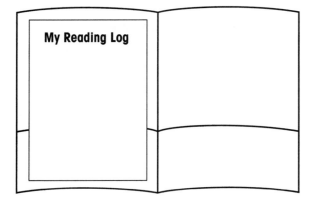

PRACTICE

1. Be sure each student has selected a book.

2. Have students log in, using information about their book.

3. As students complete this information, they should begin SQUIRT. Allow five to ten minutes for this first independent reading experience.

4. Instruct students to log out.

EXTENSION ACTIVITY

Brainstorm categories of literature—for example, fairy tales, nonfiction, mysteries, bear books, etc. Make a label for each category and place it on a box or tub. As students finish books encourage them to place them in the appropriate containers. Later the class may decide on different or additional categories and then reorganize the books accordingly.

Summarizing

OBJECTIVE
Students will be able to write a short summary of a book.

TIME FRAME: 5–10 days

ADVANCE PREPARATIONS

1. Make one copy of the Summary/Opinion & Support (S.O.S.) sheet (page 45) for each student.

2. Prepare one set of Summary Cards, (page 74)   for each group of two or three students.

BACKGROUND
Students need to be able to summarize to complete the daily S.O.S. sheet. Depending on the age and abilities of your students, you may need to repeat the lesson several times with different books.

LITERATURE SUGGESTIONS
Any high-interest literature appropriate for your students' age level will work for this lesson.

Lesson Outline

GUIDANCE
Read a book to your students and discuss what information should be included in a summary of the book. Review the difference between main ideas and details. Discuss which details would not be necessary in a summary.

Divide the class into groups of two to four students. Give each group a set of Summary Cards and a different book. Each group must keep the name of its book a secret. After reading the book, students take turns drawing a Summary Card and making an appropriate statement about the story. (In smaller groups some students may need to draw two cards.) All of the statements together will form a summary of the book. Students must decide in what order they will present their summary statements.

As each group finishes, collect the books and randomly set them on the chalk ledge. After each group presents its summary statement, the class will try to name the book.

PRACTICE

Introduce the S.O.S. sheet. Explain that students will use this form to write summaries of the books they read during SQUIRT. Each student will complete one S.O.S. sheet daily. If a student reads only part of a book in a day, the summary should relate to those pages.

Note: You may want to use the modified S.O.S. sheet (page 73) with beginning readers. Introduce it by retelling or reading *The Three Little Pigs*. Summarize the story, then model how to draw pictures to show who the main characters are in the story, what event the story was mostly about, and why it happened or how it was resolved.

Ask students to write summaries of the books they read during SQUIRT. Have students share their summaries in small groups. Use the Summary Cards to identify the important information needed in each student's summary.

EXTENSION ACTIVITIES

1. After presenting this lesson, you can begin evaluating students' S.O.S. summaries (see pages 29–31). However, delay formal grading until after you present Lesson 5, Supporting Opinions. You can prepare students for Lesson 5 as you read aloud each day. After asking students to summarize the reading selection, begin soliciting their opinions of the book and have them explain their reasoning.

2. Give each student a Summary Cards page and a 9-by-12 inch piece of manila paper. Instruct students to:

▶ Fold the manila paper into fourths

▶ Cut on the folds

▶ Fold each of the pieces into fourths again

▶ Cut on the folds

This will give each student 16 small cards. Students will use the Summary Card page as their playing board. They will not cut it apart.

Divide the class into groups of three to five students. Each student needs to list 10 to 20 books he or she has heard or read. Reproduce the Summary Spinner (page 75) for each group. Each player chooses a book from his or her list to summarize. Students take turns spinning and writing an appropriate summary statement about the chosen book on one of their cards. They read this card aloud to the group and place it on top of the corresponding Summary Card on the playing board. Then it is the next player's turn. Players forfeit a turn if the spinner lands on a summary question they've already answered.

When a player covers all of the Summary Cards on his or her board, the player calls out "Super Summary." Then the player names the chosen book, reads the summary aloud, and places the cards together to make a book. The player with the most books at the end of play or the first player to make four books is the winner.

Name _____ Date _____

S.O.S.
▼▼▼▼▼▼▼▼▼▼▼▼▼

Title _____

Author _____ Pages Read _____

Summary

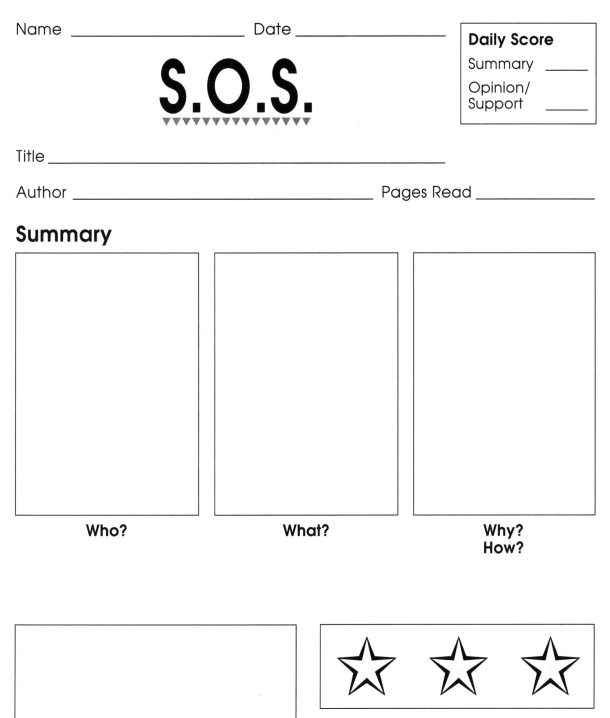

Who?   **What?**   **Why?**
                                      How?

Opinion and Support

_____

_____

_____

_____

Who?

What?

When?
Where?

Why?
How?

SUMMARY SPINNER

SPINNER DIRECTIONS:

Use a pencil and a large paper clip to make an easy, smooth-working spinner. Place the end of the paper clip over the center dot on the spinner. Keep the paper clip spinner in place by using one hand to hold the point of the pencil on the dot. Spin with the other hand.

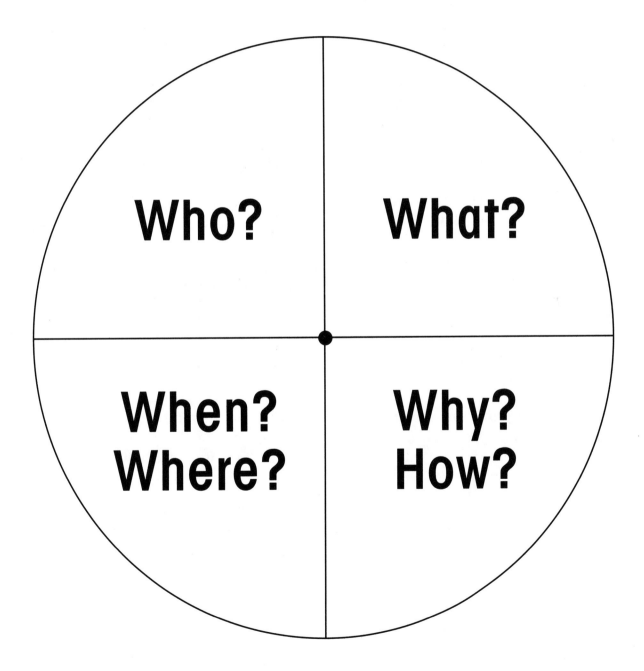

Identifying Fact and Opinion

OBJECTIVE
Students will be able to distinguish between fact and opinion.

TIME FRAME: 1–3 days

ADVANCE PREPARATIONS
Reproduce the Fact-Opinion Die found on page 78. (If you will be using the Extension Activity, also reproduce the Story Map Die.) You will need two dice for each group of three to five students.

BACKGROUND
If you have been asking students to share their opinions of your daily literature selection, they will quickly understand the difference between fact and opinion. However, be aware that when young readers agree with an opinion they hear, they frequently identify it as a fact. The more opportunities they have to discuss their own opinions and hear other opinions discussed, the clearer the differences will become.

LITERATURE SUGGESTIONS
Any humorous books appropriate to your students' age level may be used. The following suggestions have been used successfully with elementary students:

▶ *Amelia Bedelia* books by Peggy Parish
▶ *Morris Goes to School* by B. Wiseman

Lesson Outline

GUIDANCE
Read a humorous book aloud. Have volunteers summarize it. Then ask students to vote for the part they thought was funniest. Point out the many different opinions in the class. Explain the difference between fact and opinion. Make a variety of statements about the book and ask students to identify each statement as fact or opinion.

PRACTICE
Divide the class into groups of three to five students. Let each group choose a book to read. After group members have

read their book, they will take turns rolling two Fact and Opinion dice. If one die shows Fact and the other shows Opinion, the player must give a fact and an opinion statement about the book. If both dice show Fact, the player must state two facts. If both dice show Opinion, the player must state two opinions. Players score one point for each appropriate fact given and two points for each opinion. Players get zero points if their facts or opinions have already been used by a previous player. The first player to reach ten points is the winner.

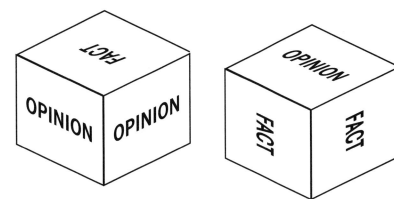

EXTENSION ACTIVITY

Make the Fact-Opinion game described in the lesson more challenging by using a Fact-Opinion die and a Story Map die. Follow the same basic procedures, except that students must make a fact or opinion statement for the specific category shown on the Story Map die.

FACT-OPINION DIE

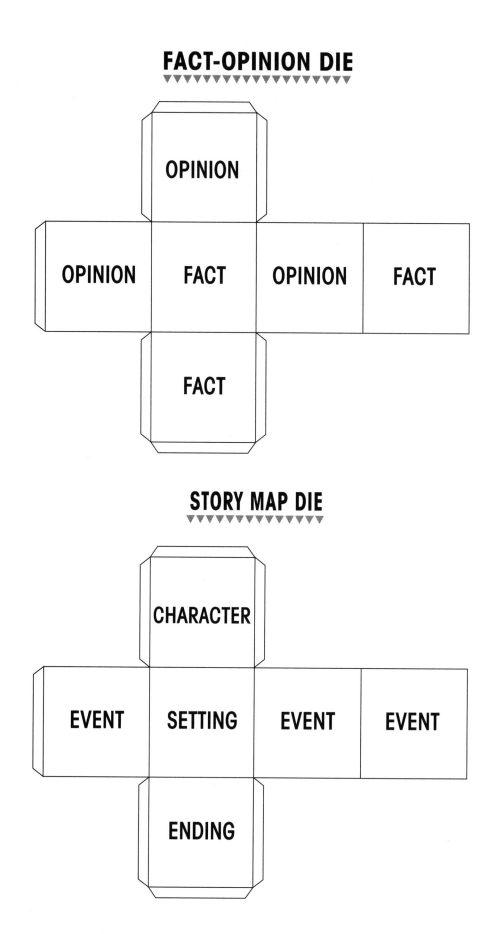

STORY MAP DIE

Supporting Opinions

OBJECTIVE

Students will be able to give an opinion and support it with details from the story or their personal experiences.

TIME FRAME: 1–3 days

ADVANCE PREPARATIONS

None needed.

BACKGROUND

The purpose of the Opinion & Support section of the S.O.S. sheet is to get students to think about why they do or do not like their reading selections. In other words, how well do they relate to the stories?

LITERATURE SUGGESTIONS

Any high-interest literature appropriate for your students' age level will work for this lesson.

Lesson Outline

GUIDANCE

Read a book aloud to your students. Ask them to summarize the story. Then review the difference between facts and opinions.

Explain that an opinion without supporting information is like a chair without legs. Give each group of three to five students a piece of paper and ask them to draw a simple chair. Next, they must make an opinion statement about the literature selection you read aloud. They write this opinion on the seat of the chair. Then they write supporting information on each leg of the chair. Share these with the class.

Little Red Riding Hood is thoughtful.

She was willing to walk a long way to visit her sick grandma.

She brought a basket of goodies to grandma.

PRACTICE

Introduce the Opinion & Support section of the S.O.S. form. Discuss the categories listed in the opinion box. Students may want to consider these aspects of their book before responding.

Ask students to reread one of their S.O.S. summaries. Next, have them think about whether or not they liked their books and why. Initially, it may be helpful to display the following sentence starter:

***I thought my book was _____
(sad, funny, scary, etc.) when . . .***

As soon as possible, remove the sentence starter and encourage students to think about how their books made them feel.

Point out that the opinion box has three stars across the top of it. Students will use these stars to rate their books. They color in all three stars if a book is excellent, two stars if it's good, and one star if it's just okay. They don't color any stars if they dislike the book.

Remind students of the Opinion Chair. Have each student write an opinion statement and give supporting reasons for it. When all students have completed this task, divide them into groups of three to five. After each student in the group has read his or her opinion statement, the group discusses whether or not the opinion was supported. If not, group members should offer suggestions and allow the student to revise the statement.

EXTENSION ACTIVITY

Play "Soup's On!" Explain that this phrase is an idiom that means that a meal is ready. Work in small groups. Each group draws a simple table on a piece of paper, then adds a large bowl sitting on the table. Students label the bowl with the title of their book. Next, have them draw a chair at each end of the table and think about the kind of discussions the book characters might have at mealtime. Label each chair with the name of a character. Students should then write an opinion from one of the characters on the seat of one chair, and another opinion from a different character on the second chair. Finally, have them list supporting information on the chair legs.

The Reading Contract

OBJECTIVE
Students will understand the procedures for completing their Reading Contract obligations.

TIME FRAME: 1 day

ADVANCE PREPARATIONS

1. Reproduce the Reading Contract (page 43). You will need one contract for each student.

2. Reproduce four S.O.S. sheets (page 45 or 73) for each student.

3. Plan a skill to teach and evaluate. Reproduce a related worksheet if necessary.

4. Assemble the Reading Contract packets. The Reading Contract goes on top, followed by four S.O.S. sheets and a skills worksheet or blank paper for recording. You may prefer to have students assemble these contract packets for themselves after this introductory lesson.

BACKGROUND
A complete discussion of the Reading Contract can be found on pages 27–31. Procedures for evaluating the S.O.S. sheet are on pages 29–31.

LITERATURE SUGGESTIONS
None needed.

Lesson Outline

GUIDANCE
Write *Contract* on the board. Explain that a contract is an agreement between two parties. The parties agree on the conditions or responsibilities named in the contract.

Hand out Reading Contract packets. Give students a few minutes to look through the packet. Then explain that this Reading Contract is an agreement between you and the students. Each week they will be responsible for completing the tasks listed on the contract. Their weekly reading grade will be determined by how well they do each task. Describe each contract responsibility. A brief explanation is all that is needed since students are already familiar with each one.

READING CONTRACT
▼▼▼▼▼▼▼▼▼▼▼▼▼▼▼▼▼▼▼▼▼▼

Name _____ Date _____

These are the things I agree to do this week: **Score**

    1. I will read _____ books/pages.   _____

    2. I will keep a daily reading log.   _____

    3. I will summarize my reading.   _____

    4. I will share my opinions about my reading.   _____

    5. I will complete the skill assignment.   _____

       Skill: _____ **Total** _____

Comments: _____

_____

_____

PRACTICE

1. Have each student set a reading goal. Demonstrate how to fill in this goal on the contract.

2. Explain and role-play the following procedures:

    A. When and where do I get a new Reading Contract each week?

    B. How do I show my reading goal?

    C. Where is the contract kept?

    D. When and where do I turn it in?

3. Point out and review the sequence of these tasks on the Flow Chart.

EXTENSION ACTIVITY

Ask students to work in small groups to write a contract for another subject such as math, science, art, or social studies. Encourage them to decide how much each responsibility should be worth. Plan a time to try out their contracts.

Reading Project: Can Do!

OBJECTIVE

Students will demonstrate story comprehension, draw conclusions, and make inferences.

TIME FRAME: 2–5 days

ADVANCE PREPARATIONS

1. Each group of three to five students will need about five index cards or 3-by-5-inch pieces of construction paper.

2. Each group will need an empty clean can for the class project. Each student will need a can for the individual project. Be sure there are no sharp edges on the open end of the cans.

BACKGROUND

This activity focuses the students' attention on the relationship between different story events and their effect on particular characters. Students should have had Skills lesson 4, Story Mapping, before you present this Reading Project. They may also need Skills lessons on paraphrasing, writing quotations, drawing conclusions, and making inferences.

LITERATURE SUGGESTIONS

Miss Nelson Is Missing by Harry Allard and James Marshall

Sarah, Plain and Tall by Patricia MacLachlan

Amelia Bedelia by Peggy Parish

Amos and Boris by William Steig

Mufaro's Beautiful Daughters by John Steptoe

Sleeping Ugly by Jane Yolen

Lesson Outline

GUIDANCE

Read a book with strong character development. Summarize the story and solicit students' opinions about each character.

Make a class story map of the book you read. Explain that students will be looking at the way a particular character is affected by each aspect of the story map. Draw cans on the board and label them *Can Do, Can See, Can Say or Think, Can Hear,* and *Can Feel.*

Decide which character to use in the

class Can Do! project. Assign each group a "can" category. According to each group's assigned category, students write five to ten statements that describe what the character can do, see, say or think, hear, or feel. Group members should write each statement on an index card and place it in their can. Then they work together to design and make a story label for their can.

When all groups have finished, have them share their Can Do! cans. Discuss the details or clues from the stories that helped them reach their conclusions about the characters.

PRACTICE

1. Each student chooses a book and writes Can Do! statements for each category about one of the characters.

2. Each student then designs a story label and places the statement cards in the can.

3. Declare a Produce Day when students share their cans.

EXTENSION ACTIVITY

Use a rubber band to hold each student's Can Do! cards from the lesson together. Put all of the sets of cards in a large class can labeled *Can You "Can Do"?* Set out each student's story can. Students read a set of cards and place them in the appropriate story can.

Reading Project: Peek Overs

OBJECTIVE
Students will demonstrate comprehension by comparing and contrasting two literature selections.

TIME FRAME: 2–5 days

ADVANCE PREPARATIONS

1. Each student needs two pieces of 12-by-18-inch construction paper, and glue.

2. Make tagboard Peek Over patterns (see page 88). Students will trace these on manila paper and decorate them to make story characters. Make a poster showing different characters. Students can refer to this poster for ideas.

BACKGROUND
This activity focuses on similarities and differences. Younger students may need to concentrate on character traits, while older students may prefer investigating themes (friendship, journeys, treasures, etc.) or styles of writing (fairy tales, poetry, etc.).

Model the use of lists, charts, and Venn diagrams to record the comparisons of two books. This will give students a variety of choices for recording their own information.

LITERATURE SUGGESTIONS
Any two literature selections with similar characters, plots, or themes can be used with this activity. The following books are organized by character, theme, or genre:

Fables and Fairy Tales
Fables by Arnold Lobel

Just So Stories by Rudyard Kipling

Sleeping Beauty by Trina Schart Hyman

Sleeping Ugly by Jane Yolen

Snow White by The Brothers Grimm

Friendship
Best Friends by Steven Kellogg

Amos and Boris by William Steig

Rosie and Michael by Judith Viorst

Frog and Toad Are Friends by Arnold Lobel

Alexander and the Wind-Up Mouse by Leo Lionni

Swimmy by Leo Lionni

Journeys

Henry the Explorer by Mark Taylor

The Island of the Skog by Steven Kellogg

The Ox-Cart Man by Donald Hall

Bears

Little Bear by Else Holmelund Minarik

Goldilocks and The Three Bears by Jan Brett

Deep in the Forest by Brinton Turkle

The Berenstain Bears series by Jan and Stan Berenstain

Corduroy by Don Freeman

Pigs

Chester the Worldly Pig by Bill Peet

Pigs Might Fly by Dick King-Smith

Roland the Minstrel Pig by William Steig

A Treeful of Pigs by Arnold Lobel

Lesson Outline

GUIDANCE

Read two literature selections with similar characters, plots, themes, or genres. Summarize each selection and share opinions about the two stories. Then make a class chart or Venn diagram comparing ways the two stories are similar and different.

PRACTICE

1. Give students two pieces of construction paper. Instruct them to fold each piece in half. Then they fold under about one inch on one end of each paper, to form a flap on each piece. They glue the flap of one paper to the unfolded end of the other paper. Finally they glue the remaining flap in place to form a bottomless and topless box.

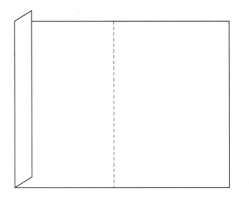

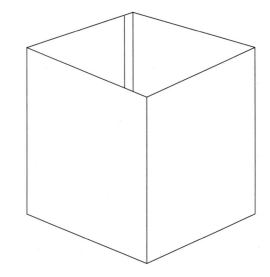

2. Write and illustrate a summary of each book on two pages. Glue the pages on two sides of the box.

3. Label another page "Similarities." List ways the two books are alike. Decorate and glue this to another side of the box.

4. Repeat step 3 to make a "Differences" page for the remaining side.

5. Create Peek Over story characters to decorate the top of the box.

EXTENSION ACTIVITY

This activity requires a higher level of thinking. Students must find similarities between two dissimilar books.

Display ten to twenty books. Choose a variety, avoiding those with obvious similarities. Write the name of each book on an index card and place the cards in a paper bag. Without looking, students must draw two cards. After reading the two books, they record similarities and differences and prepare a Peek Over using this information.

PEEK OVER PATTERN

Reading Project: Point of View

OBJECTIVE

Students will show appreciation for different viewpoints by retelling a story from another character's point of view.

TIME FRAME: 2–5 days

ADVANCE PREPARATIONS

1. Each group of students will need one die.

2. Make a viewpoint spinner for the book you will be reading aloud. Divide an index card in half. Draw a sketch or write the name of a different character on each half. Add a spinner.

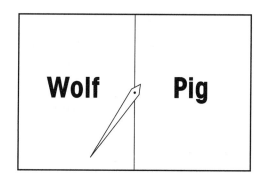

BACKGROUND

This is an excellent follow-up activity to the Can Do! Reading Project. It helps

students challenge their preconceived ideas about a character or event and look at each from a different perspective. To accomplish this, students must examine possible underlying feelings and attitudes of characters they have commonly accepted as villains.

LITERATURE SUGGESTIONS

Any literature selection that presents a well-known story from a different point of view will be appropriate.

The Jolly Postman by Janet and Allan Ahlberg

The Big Orange Splot by Daniel Manus Pinkwater

Ben and Me or *Captain Kidd's Cat* by Robert Lawson

The True Story of the 3 Little Pigs by Jon Scieszka

Lesson Outline

GUIDANCE

Read one of the literature suggestions aloud. Compare the character's point of

THE TRUE STORY OF THE 3 LITTLE PIGS
▼▼▼▼▼▼▼▼▼▼▼▼▼▼▼▼▼▼▼▼▼▼▼▼▼▼▼▼▼

	Pigs	Wolf
1. Setting:	pig's private home	neighbor's house
2. Characters:	wolf is an enemy	pigs are neighbors
3. First Event:	wolf attacks	sneezes
4. Second Event:	wolf attacks again	cold gets worse
5. Third Event:	wolf tries to attack	pig insults wolf
6. Ending:	calls police	unjustly imprisoned

view to the traditional version of the story. Discuss the validity of the characters' viewpoints: Do both points of view make sense? Are there details to support both arguments?

Make a class list of six story elements that could be viewed from different perspectives. These might include setting, time, first event, second event, third event, and ending. (See example above.)

Give each small group of students a die and a viewpoint spinner. On their turn, players will spin the spinner and roll the die. This will determine which viewpoint they will give on what story element. For example, if the spinner lands on Wolf and the student rolls a 4, he or she must make an appropriate statement reflecting the wolf's viewpoint of his visit to the second pig's house. Make a chart to record the groups' statements on each element. They may have more than one character statement for an element. Share the statements with the class.

PRACTICE
Ask each student to read a story and think about the events from a different point of view. Have each student design a chart to compare two characters' viewpoints on several events in the story.

EXTENSION ACTIVITY
Stage a mock trial of a character. Explain that in the United States an individual accused of a wrongdoing is considered innocent until proven guilty. Choose one team of lawyers to defend an accused character's actions and another team to prosecute. Assign students to be witnesses, jurors, and judge.

Make a class chart labeled *Prosecution* and *Defense*. As the jury hears the lawyers present both sides of the case, assign a point for each appropriate argument for or against the character. They will then find the character guilty or not guilty. If the character is found guilty, the judge will consult with the jury and decide on an appropriate punishment. The punishment must fit the crime. It must be nonviolent, help the character learn a lesson, and right his or her wrong.

Reading Project: Game Boards

OBJECTIVE

Students will demonstrate story sequencing and comprehension by developing a game board.

TIME FRAME: 2–5 days

ADVANCE PREPARATIONS

1. Provide an assortment of construction paper for game boards.

2. Have an assortment of buttons available for use as markers.

BACKGROUND

A linear story begins at one point and ends at another. A circular story begins and ends at the same point. *If You Give a Mouse a Cookie* by Laura Joffe Numeroff is an example of a circular story plot.

Read several examples of each kind of story to prepare students for this activity. Discuss and illustrate the plot pattern of each story.

Linear story plots lend themselves to game-board layouts like Candy Land. Circular story plots go best with game-board layouts like Monopoly.

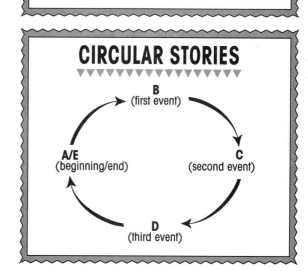

LINEAR STORIES
▼▼▼▼▼▼▼▼▼▼▼▼▼

A (beginning)
B (first event)
C (second event)
D (third event)
E (ending)

CIRCULAR STORIES
▼▼▼▼▼▼▼▼▼▼▼▼▼

B (first event)
C (second event)
D (third event)
A/E (beginning/end)

LITERATURE SUGGESTIONS

Any high-interest literature appropriate for your students' age level will work well for this lesson. The following books have circular plots:

The Ox-Cart Man by Donald Hall

Drummer Hoff by Barbara Emberley

Where the Wild Things Are by Maurice Sendak

GAME BOARDS

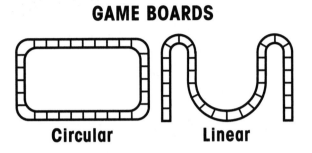

Circular   Linear

Lesson Outline

GUIDANCE

Read two books, one with a linear and one with a circular plot. After reading each book aloud, ask volunteers to summarize the story.

Make a list of board games students enjoy playing. Explain the difference between linear and circular game boards. Ask students to think about the two literature selections they heard. Which story plot would best match each kind of game board and why?

PRACTICE

1. Working individually or in small groups, students read a book and then create a game around the story. Have construction paper available for boards and other game pieces. The game board should reflect the characters and show the main events in proper sequence. Depending on the story, it may have a circular or linear design.

2. Students should decide whether to use a spinner, dice, or task cards.

3. When the game is finished, students must write clear directions for the game and try it out with several other students.

EXTENSION ACTIVITY

Have a Game Day. Divide the class into groups of three to five students. Ask students to share summaries of their game board books with the group. Then have each child explain the rules of the game so the group can play it. Take turns until each student in the group has shared a game.

Lead a class discussion on the attributes of a fun game (clear directions, fast movement, an element of risk, etc.). Then allow students to revise their games. If time permits, divide the class into different groups and play again using the revisions.

Getting Started:
SKILLS LESSONS

Keeping a Journal

OBJECTIVE

Students will record their feelings, impressions, and observations in a writer's journal.

TIME FRAME: 1–2 days

ADVANCE PREPARATIONS

1. Choose a book from Literature Suggestions or any other diary or journal-type book to read to your students.

2. Help students assemble their Writer's Journals. Any format that's appealing and easy to use will be appropriate. The following journals require minimum preparation time and can easily be stored in the students' writing folders:

    A. spiral notebooks or steno pads

    B. notebook or tablet paper bound in three-prong folders

    C. writing paper stapled between construction paper covers

    D. writing paper fastened to a file folder (see Extension Activity)

BACKGROUND

It is important that students view these journals as more than just anecdotal records. The focus should be on their feelings, impressions, and observations. A student may write about one idea one day and the next day write about something totally unrelated. The journal is the students' practice field—a place to experiment with the sound of their thoughts and feelings. Sometimes they will like the results and want to turn their entries into complete stories. Other times they will lose interest and abandon their ideas.

Initially you may want to spend a few minutes each day inviting volunteers to read their entries. Rather than calling on all volunteers, request specific information. For example, share an entry that describes something you saw (felt, heard, etc.). Then have the class make summary statements about the feelings or impression shared by the students and discuss possible ways the entries might be used as the basis of stories.

LITERATURE SUGGESTIONS

Joshua's Westward Journal by Joan Anderson

Arthur's Pen Pal by Lillian Hoban

The Diary of a Church Mouse by Graham Oakley

Stringbean's Trip to the Shining Sea by Vera Williams

Three Days on a River in a Red Canoe by Vera Williams

Lesson Outline

GUIDANCE

Read a diary or journal-type book and discuss the kinds of feelings, impressions, and observations the character shares through his or her entry.

Explain that students will begin each Independent Work period by writing in their Writer's Journal. Remind them to write like a writer. In other words, they must do more than just tell what happened. They must share feelings, impressions, and observations about the event.

PRACTICE

Allow about five minutes for students to write entries in their journals. Ask volunteers to read their journal entries, and have the class summarize the thoughts and feelings shared in the entries. Discuss different ways the entries might be expanded into complete stories.

Show students the task labeled Writer's Journal on the Flow Chart bulletin board. From now on they will begin Independent Work time by writing in their journals. Throughout the year they will be looking back at these journal entries. When they work on Writing Projects, they may decide to turn some of the entries into complete stories.

EXTENSION ACTIVITIES

1. At various age levels students are often required to learn specific styles of writing. You can meaningfully incorporate these required skills into their self-selected writing. For example, after a lesson on descriptive writing, you might ask students to look through their journals and find one entry each that they can make more descriptive. You can use these entries to evaluate how successfully students have learned to apply the writing components you have been teaching.

2. Students can assemble and decorate their own Writer's Journals. Each student will need a file folder, one brad, and writing paper. With the folder opened flat, they fasten the paper to the top left corner of the right side of the file folder. Using a single brad allows students to comfortably turn the pages of their journals up and out of the way to write on a new page. Cut off the file folder tab so the journal will fit into the Writing Folder.

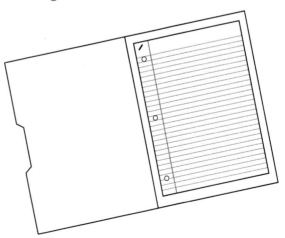

Combine an art lesson on line design with the construction of these journals to create interesting, personalized covers. First, discuss different types of lines: straight, curved, jagged, dots, dashes, waves, etc. Give students paper and let them practice using each type of line to make a pattern.

Have each student draw a border near the edges of the cover. This should be freehand, with either square or rounded corners. Instruct each child to add another border about one inch (or two finger spaces) inside the first one.

Next, ask each student to:

▶ Draw his or her initial or a simple object in the center of the cover;

▶ Draw ten to twelve lines radiating out from the initial or object to the border;

▶ Fill each space formed by these radiating lines with a different line pattern. Students may either use their practice patterns or experiment with new ones.

Not only are these journals fun and easy to assemble, they are also easily maintained throughout the year. Students can add writing pages as needed. Most important, they can remove journal entries they want to develop into complete stories. This makes a journal not merely a collection of thoughts but an effective writing tool.

Finding Topics

OBJECTIVE

Students will generate a list of writing topics.

TIME FRAME: 1 day

ADVANCE PREPARATIONS

1. Each student needs a pocket folder. These will be used to prepare individual Writing Folders (see page 26).

2. Select one of the literature suggestions to read aloud.

3. Duplicate a copy of Brainstorms (page 99) for each student.

BACKGROUND

After this lesson, students will prepare their Writing Folders and attach their Brainstorms topic list on the inside. This should become an ongoing list. As students develop new interests and experience different events in their lives, they will add writing topics to the list.

LITERATURE SUGGESTIONS

Judith Viorst is the focus author. Her writing topics come from her own experiences or those of her three children.

Alexander and the Terrible, Horrible, No Good, Very Bad Day

Alexander, Who Used to Be Rich Last Sunday

Earrings

If I Were in Charge of the World and Other Worries

Rosie and Michael

Lesson Outline

GUIDANCE

Read a Judith Viorst selection and discuss how she might have come up with her ideas. Explain that Judith Viorst has written and published many children's books and several poetry books. She usually writes about the feelings and events that happen to her own children, Alexander, Anthony, and Nicholas. Like all good writers, she writes about the things she knows best.

Have students work in groups of three to five to brainstorm possible writing topics. These should be subjects or events the students know well, such as specific things they like to do, feelings, people, or pets in their lives. Allow five to ten minutes for the groups to discuss ideas.

Invite each student to share one idea with the class. Encourage them to listen carefully to avoid repeating an idea that has already been suggested. Record these ideas on the board. Continue until all ideas have been shared, or until there is no more space for recording.

PRACTICE

Give each student a copy of the Brainstorms page. Ask students to choose five to ten of their favorite writing topics, taking them all from the board if they wish. They should list these topics on the Brainstorms page and then, as time permits, draw idea pictures in the frame. These should be sketches or doodles of people, pets, or objects they know well and might want to use in future writing.

EXTENSION ACTIVITY

1. Use the Topic Chart (page 100) in place of the Brainstorms page, or save it for later in the year as an additional source of writing topics.

2. Begin an Author Spotlight bulletin board. Periodically highlight a different author. Display a picture of the author, a variety of his or her books, and a brief background—including any information about the sources of his or her topics. *Instructor* magazine as well as many of the monthly children's book clubs (available through schools) feature different authors each month. These often provide the teacher with a picture and information about the author.

Brainstorms!

TOPIC CHART
▼▼▼▼▼▼▼▼▼▼▼▼▼▼

People I Know	Feelings I Have
Places I've Been	**Things I Think About**
Things I've Done	**Special Ideas**

The Writing Process

OBJECTIVE

Students will understand that writing goes through a variety of steps before the initial idea becomes a finished piece of writing.

TIME FRAME: 1–2 days

ADVANCE PREPARATIONS

1. Choose an author to highlight. (See Literature Suggestions.)

2. Reproduce the Writing Process Pencil (page 104) for each student.

3. Cut a 4-by-9-inch strip of construction paper or tagboard for each student. The Writing Process Pencil will be mounted on this.

4. Cut a 12-inch piece of yarn or ribbon for each student.

5. For younger students, you may want to punch the hole in the pocket of each Writing Folder ahead of time. (See Practice #6.)

BACKGROUND

Good writing goes through several steps as it progresses from the author's original idea to a polished piece of writing ready to be shared by others. The purpose of writing is to communicate ideas. Each step of the writing process helps make the author's idea easier to understand. When students see the different stages of their writing as important, necessary steps forward, they become less resistant to revising and editing.

LITERATURE SUGGESTIONS

Stan and Jan Berenstain's Bear books are based on ideas from everyday experiences. It takes the authors about six months to complete a book, and during this time their story and illustrations go through many, many revisions.

The Carrot Seed by Ruth Krauss. This book began as a 10,000-word story and was revised and simplified to its present 100 words. The idea came from an imaginary conversation she had with her five-year-old neighbor.

The Paper Bag Princess and *Moira's Birthday* by Robert Munsch. At first

Munsch was reluctant to try writing because he was such a poor speller, but then he figured out that writing was not the same as spelling. He tells his stories over and over about 100 times before he writes them down. Each time he retells a story he revises it. Then he writes it down and does his final revisions.

Lesson Outline

GUIDANCE

Read one of the suggested literature selections or any other book for which you can provide a brief story background. Tell as much as possible about the process the author went through in writing the story.

Explain that whether you are writing a story, designing a poster, or composing a song, all writing goes through several changes before it is ready for others to read. These changes are called the writing process. Not everyone thinks through this process in exactly the same way, but we all go through the same basic steps. Explain that students will use these steps as a guide to produce their best possible writing. Tell students that over the next few weeks they'll be exploring each step in greater detail.

Briefly discuss each of the following steps as you list them on the board or point to them on your Flow Chart bulletin board:

▶ **Story Map:** This is a plan or outline that names the main ideas in your writing. It will help you think ahead about what you want to say. As you write, it will help you stick to your topic.

▶ **Rough Draft:** At this stage you want to get your ideas down quickly. Don't worry about spelling, punctuation, or neatness, as long as you can read your own work.

▶ **Peer Conference:** Choose two peers whom you trust to give you advice on your rough draft. Then read your draft out loud to them. Discuss what they like and what you might change to make your story better.

▶ **Revise:** You now work to make your story better. You may want to use some of the suggestions you heard in your peer conference, or you may have ideas of your own to try out.

▶ **Edit:** When you feel happy with your revised writing, check it for spelling and punctuation errors.

▶ **Layout:** Decide how you want to publish your writing and what materials you will need. Plan what will go on each page and where you want to illustrate.

▶ **Publish:** Use your layout plans to recopy and illustrate your writing so that other students can enjoy it. (Students may not choose to publish everything they write; see page 40.)

PRACTICE

1. Give each student one Writing Process Pencil page. Have them cut out the pencil and the box of writing process steps.

2. Explain that the writing process steps are not in order. Students should cut them apart and lay them on the pencil in the correct order.

3. Check students' work either individually or as a whole class. Have them rearrange any pieces that are out of order and glue them in place.

4. Have each child cut out the box of editing marks and glue it to the back of the pencil. Explain that you will discuss these editing marks in detail in a later Skills lesson.

5. Have students use crayons or markers to decorate their pencils.

6. Have (or help) each child punch a hole in the pencil as indicated. Attach a 12-inch piece of ribbon or yarn to the pencil. Punch a hole in the pocket of the student's Writing Folder and attach the other end to the folder. Students will use this as a reference throughout the year. It can be laminated or covered with clear contact paper for added durability.

EXTENSION ACTIVITY

Make Writing Process Cards. Put each of the following steps on a separate index card: Story Map, Rough Draft, Peer Conference, Revise, Edit, Layout, Publish. You may also want to add a Choose to Publish card to reinforce when this decision will be made. You will need enough sets of cards so that each student can receive at least one card. Make each set of cards a different color or add distinguishing marks or stickers.

Shuffle all the sets of Writing Process Cards together. Give one card to each student. If there are extra cards, you may need to give some students two cards. If so, make sure that they get two cards from the same set. When you say "Go," the students will quickly get themselves together in appropriate groups and stand so that the cards they are holding show the writing process steps in order. Students holding more than one card are free to exchange cards with someone in their group so they can hold two consecutive cards.

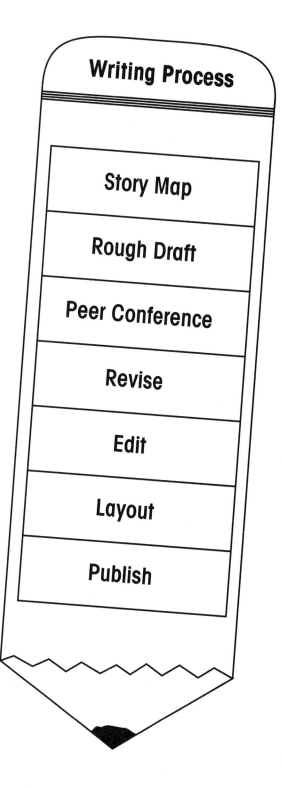

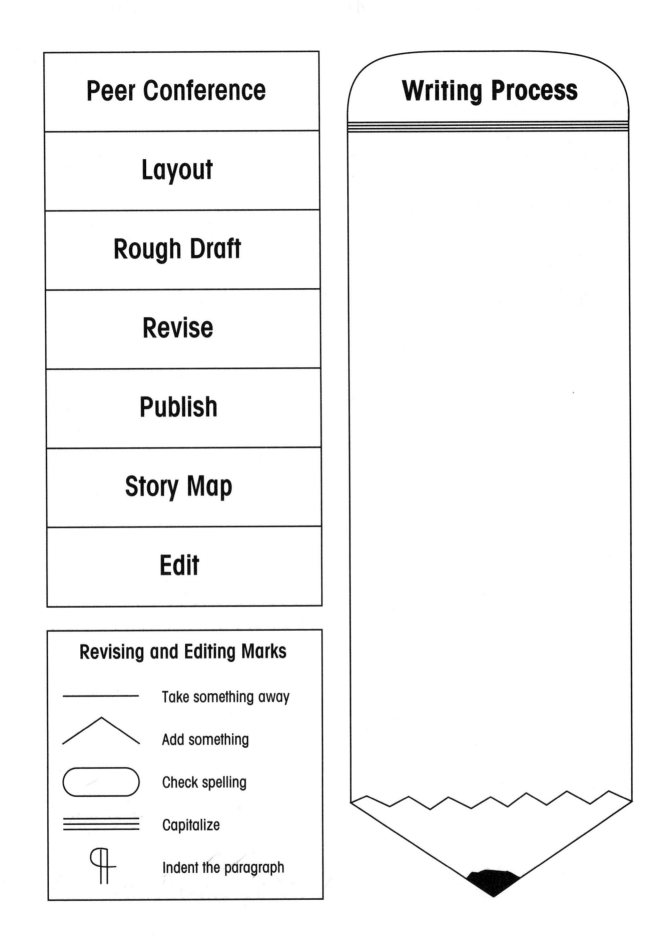

Peer Conference

Layout

Rough Draft

Revise

Publish

Story Map

Edit

Writing Process

Revising and Editing Marks

—————— Take something away

⋀ Add something

⬭ Check spelling

☰ Capitalize

¶ Indent the paragraph

Story Mapping

OBJECTIVE

Students will be able to use prewriting strategies to organize thoughts for writing.

TIME FRAME: 1–2 days

ADVANCE PREPARATIONS

1. Choose a snapshot of yourself that can be the basis of a story.

2. Each student should try to bring a snapshot from home. The student should be in the picture, and it should show an activity or event that the student would like to write about. If students forget or are unable to bring a snapshot, provide time for them to draw a picture of an event to share. They should put their drawing on snapshot-size paper.

3. Enlarge and reproduce the Story Map master (page 108). You'll display this for reference all year.

4. Each student will need writing paper.

BACKGROUND

This story mapping activity begins a project that will continue in Skills lessons 5 to 10.

Writing without a plan is like trying to work a jigsaw puzzle without looking at the picture on the puzzle box. It can be done, but it definitely takes much more effort! Students need to be taught to think before they write. Completing story maps forces them to consider and plan the beginning, middle, and end of their stories.

Although there are many different story map formats, all these choices can leave young writers feeling overwhelmed. Therefore only one format is presented. It can be applied to all types of writing (descriptive, narrative, etc.).

By adding arms, feet, and other features, you can decorate the story map to look like a person or a robot. This may further serve to help students remember the basic components of a piece of writing.

Remind students that this Story Map is a tool to help them become better writers. There may be times when the story they want to tell does not perfectly fit the map. For example, there may be only two events in their story. That's all right. The story map is a guide and not a law.

LITERATURE SUGGESTIONS

Any high-interest book appropriate for your grade level will work for this lesson. Read the book in advance and be prepared, if necessary, to lead students to generalizations that will help them see how the parts of the book fit the story map.

Lesson Outline

GUIDANCE

Pass around a snapshot of yourself and explain what was happening when the picture was taken. Be sure to include information about other people or animals in the picture, where the picture was taken, and what happened. You are modeling the parts of a story.

Introduce the story map poster to the class. Point out that a good story has a beginning that lets the reader know what the story will be about, a middle that describes the events, and a conclusion that tells how things turn out.

Model this by completing a story map for your snapshot story. The focus should be on telling the idea (characters, setting, etc.) with single words or brief phrases. Explain that, just like a road map, a story map shows the direction the story is taking, but it does not describe everything that you will see along the way.

PRACTICE

1. Students work in groups of three or

four. Each student has a snapshot or a drawing of some event that he or she wants to tell about. Allow about ten minutes for students to share their pictures with the members of their group and tell what was happening. Encourage students to include all the parts from the story map.

2. Students independently complete a story map for their own picture.

3. They share these story maps with their group.

4. They save the story maps in their Writing Folders for use with Skills lessons 5 to 10.

EXTENSION ACTIVITIES

1. Depending on the amount of reading and writing experience your students have, they may need further practice before they are ready to make their own story maps.

▶ Read a book aloud and make a class story map for the book. You may need to repeat this activity several times to help students see the relationship between the different parts of the story map and the actual book.

▶ Read a book aloud and ask students to work with a partner or small group to make a Story Map for the book. When everyone is finished, discuss their responses for the different parts of the story map.

▶ Read a book aloud and ask students to make a story map for the book independently. Discuss their responses.

2. Play Story Map Clue. Students work

in groups of three or four to write one or two story maps for well-known stories. They must keep the name of their book(s) a secret. When each group has this completed, the class is ready to begin. You will need to prepare one 8-space spinner for the class. Write each part of the story map in the spinner spaces.

The object of the game is to guess the name of the book. Each group takes a turn being the game-show hosts and presenting their story map clues. The remaining groups are the contestant teams who take turns spinning the story map spinner.

The spinner determines which story map clue is revealed. For example, if the spinner lands on Setting, the host group gives the story setting. (All teams get to hear all the clues that are revealed.) If the spinner lands on a clue that has already been revealed, the team does not get to spin again but may try to guess the name of the book using the clues already known. In either case, the team has 30 seconds to make a guess.

The first team to guess the name of the book for which the story map was written wins the game and they become the next game-show hosts. Continue until all groups have had a turn.

STORY MAP

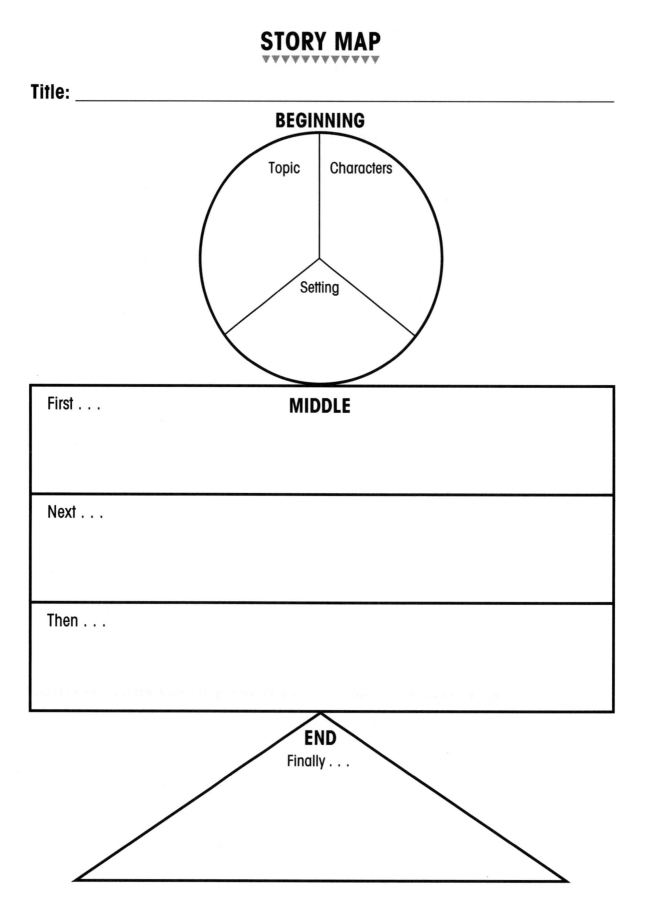

Title: _____

BEGINNING

Topic

Characters

Setting

MIDDLE

First . . .

Next . . .

Then . . .

END

Finally . . .

Rough Draft: Beginning a Story

OBJECTIVE

Students will be able to write story beginnings that establish an appropriate focus for their readers.

TIME FRAME: 1–2 days

ADVANCE PREPARATIONS

1. Make one window book pattern for every four to five students. Cut tagboard to the size of the notebook or tablet paper your students will be using. Draw and cut a 3 $\frac{1}{4}$-inch square centered in the top half of the page. The snapshot will show through this square when the project is completed. The students will write on the bottom half of the page.

2. Prepare a piece of window paper to use for recording the story beginning that you will be modeling.

BACKGROUND

Spelling can become a stumbling block to fluent writing. First, teach students that there are two kinds of acceptable spelling. *Standard spelling* is used in publishing, where words are spelled in commonly accepted ways. *Functional spelling*, also known as invented spelling, uses the sounds heard in a word and allows a writer to get his or her ideas down without stopping to worry about standard spelling for unknown words. Both standard and functional spelling can play a part in writing.

LITERATURE SUGGESTIONS

Any high-interest books, especially those with interesting or unusual beginnings. You will need four to ten in all.

Lesson Outline

GUIDANCE

Ask students to think what makes them want to continue reading a book they just started. Then read the opening lines of four to ten books to your class. After each opening ask the class whether they would like to hear the rest of the story. Discuss why or why not.

Explain that a story beginning gets readers interested and helps them know about the characters, setting, and topic of the story. Remind students of the many different ways they just heard authors begin their books.

Now use your snapshot to model the student activity. Write a beginning to the story of your snapshot. Demonstrate how you could start your story another way by writing a second, completely different beginning. Then write a third story beginning. Try to make each one as unique and interesting as possible.

Have the students work in small groups to discuss which of three beginnings is most interesting and makes them want to hear more of the story. Discuss the different opinions.

PRACTICE

1. Ask students to look at their snapshots and think about the stories they want to tell. Have them use their story maps, to write beginnings for their stories. Tell them to skip a space after each line they write. This will make it easier for them to revise and edit later.

2. Have them reread their beginnings. Did they let the reader know about the characters, setting, and topic of the story?

3. Following the procedures you modeled, each student should write a second and then a third story beginning. They should try to make each story beginning as interesting and unique as possible.

4. Working in groups of three or four, students take turns reading their story beginnings. After each writer shares, the group should discuss which beginning is most interesting and makes them want to hear more about the snapshot.

5. Allow time for each student to choose his or her best beginning. Point out that this is a revising step. The students have just made a choice which will help make their story easier to understand.

6. Have each student work with a partner to edit. First, have the pairs check to be sure that their sentences begin with capital letters and end with periods. Then have them find and circle misspelled words. While students may not know the correct spellings they will often recognize misspelled words. Have them use the following procedures to find the correct spellings:

    A. First, try it. Students spell the word functionally, using as many sounds as they can hear.

    B. Second, look it up. Students think of logical places to find a word in print—such as on a wall chart, in a library or text book, or on a class bulletin board. Older children will be able to look up words in a dictionary. Younger children may want to make individual or class dictionaries with words they need to spell.

    C. Third, ask a peer. If students have tried unsuccessfully to look up words, they may ask other students in the class.

    D. Fourth, ask a teacher. Use only when all else fails.

7. Have each student trace and cut out a window page. Then have students use their best handwriting to recopy the first page of their window books on the bottom half of the page. They should save their rough drafts and final copies in their Writing Folders.

Window Page

EXTENSION ACTIVITY

Authors use a number of techniques to capture and hold the reader's interest. The techniques they use largely depend on their purpose in writing. As you read to your students, begin collecting examples of different ways authors get and keep their readers' interest. Throughout the year, present examples of these different techniques and discuss their effect upon the reader. Invite your students to experiment with these techniques in their own writing. There will be a noticeable difference in their writing once they begin to read books from a writer's point of view.

Each of the following writing techniques could become the focus of later lessons:

▶ **Description:** The author paints a word picture that gives visual details about a character, setting, emotion, or event.

▶ **Naming:** The author gives specific information about people, places, or times. Instead of "The boy was late to school," the author might write "Michael was now ten minutes late to Mrs. McKay's first period math class."

▶ **Suspense:** The author provides just enough information to heighten the reader's curiosity.

▶ **Surprise:** Carefully chosen details are left out of the story, leading the reader to make incorrect assumptions. Then, later in the story, the author reveals the surprise element.

▶ **Repetition:** The author repeats words or phrases throughout the plot. "Run, run as fast as you can. You can't catch me. I'm the gingerbread man."

▶ **Dialogue or Monologue:** The author uses conversation between characters or between a character and him- or herself to reveal information about the plot.

▶ **Flashback:** The author takes the reader back to an earlier time. This technique is often used to help the reader understand a character's motivation for a later action.

▶ **Comparison:** The author compares two characters, settings, or events to show how alike or different they are.

Rough Draft: Continuing the Story

OBJECTIVE
Students will be able to use a story map to write a rough draft.

TIME FRAME: 2–3 days

ADVANCE PREPARATIONS
None. (Students will continue using the snapshot and story map referred to in Skills lesson 4.)

BACKGROUND
Writing a rough draft requires different thinking and different skills from writing a story map. Students who are having difficulty mastering these skills often need to learn elaboration techniques. They may also benefit from using their story maps to help them *tell* their stories to peers before they try to *write* them.

A controlled peer conference is planned for this lesson. It is intended to be an introductory experience. The focus will be on reading rough drafts and inviting positive peer comments. Complete peer conference etiquette and procedures will be presented in Skills lesson 8.

LITERATURE SUGGESTIONS
Any high-interest literature appropriate for your students' age level will work for this lesson.

Lesson Outline

GUIDANCE
Make a class story map for a familiar book on the board. Then ask students to think about how the author described the setting, characters, and events as they listen to you read the book aloud.

Discuss some of the interesting language or writing techniques the author used to describe the setting, characters, and events. Compare this to the story map. Retell the story to demonstrate how different it would have sounded if the author had just used simple sentences to tell the story map information:

▶ *The characters in this story are . . .*

▶ *It takes place in . . .*

▶ *The purpose of this story is to tell you about . . .*

▶ *First . . . (first event)*

▶ *Next . . . (second event)*

▶ *Then . . . (third event)*

▶ *Finally . . . (how the story problem was resolved)*

A story map is much like the skeleton of a puppy. The skeleton determines its size and shape, but it's the puppy's muscle, skin, and fur that make it soft, warm, and cuddly. A story map determines the direction or shape of a story, but the words the author chooses for the rough draft make the story alive and exciting.

PRACTICE

1. Remind students that the story beginning they wrote in Skills lesson 5 was the first part of their rough draft. Now they'll use their story map to continue writing the rough draft. This time they will be writing about the events in their stories.

2. Working in groups of two or three, students should take turns reading their rough drafts. After each turn, the group will discuss interesting words and sentences that the author used to tell about one or more story map parts.

3. After these peer conferences, allow time for each student to make necessary revisions.

4. Invite students to share parts of their rough drafts with the class, selecting their most interesting description(s) of characters, setting, or events.

EXTENSION ACTIVITY

Choose a plainly written book—such as a simple version of a familiar folk- or fairy tale—to read aloud to your students. Make a class story map. Challenge students to use the information on the story map to rewrite a more elaborate and more interesting version. Make these into illustrated books and share them with another class.

Rough Draft: Concluding a Story

OBJECTIVE

Students will be able to distinguish between a story's final event, how the problem or conflict was resolved, and the closing or "happily ever after" statement.

TIME FRAME: 1–3 days

ADVANCE PREPARATIONS

None. (Students will continue using the snapshot and rough draft referred to in Skills lesson 4.)

BACKGROUND

Often, students do not understand the difference between a story's climax and the closing or resolution statement. Many students see the climax as the end of the story. Consequently they often end their own stories too abruptly.

LITERATURE SUGGESTIONS

Choose three to five high-interest books. You will be reading aloud only the last line of each book, so be sure that your students are familiar with the basic plot.

Lesson Outline

GUIDANCE

Display three to five familiar books. Ask students to briefly retell the plot of each story. Focus on the story problem and how it is resolved. Explain that this problem resolution is also called the climax of the story. (Option: Divide the class into small groups and let each group discuss the plots among themselves.)

When students have discussed all the books, read the last line of each book to your class. Lead students to see how these final sentences let the reader know whether or not the characters lived happily ever after.

Students should understand that the conclusion of a story has two parts. The climax tells how the story problem is resolved, and the closing, or happily-ever-after statement, summarizes a lesson the characters learned, restates the main idea, or simply lets the reader know that the characters went on with their lives.

Use your snapshot to model the

student activity. Read your rough draft to the students. Have them identify the characters, setting, events, and climax. Next, write a happily-ever-after statement for your picture, such as "We were all so tired that we went straight to bed as soon as we got home" or "It was the best vacation I have ever had."

Next, ask the students to work in small groups to brainstorm several possible happily-ever-after statements for their snapshots.

PRACTICE

1. Have students add happily-ever-after statements to their rough drafts.

2. Ask them to reread their rough drafts from beginning to end. They should read them slowly and softly to themselves, listening carefully to be sure that what they wrote makes sense and says what they meant it to say. They should make any revisions they need.

EXTENSION ACTIVITY

Read one of Aesop's fables to your students. Point out that the moral or lesson at the end of each fable is the closing or happily-ever-after statement. Read aloud another fable, but do not read the moral. Let the students write this closing statement.

Peer Conference and Revising

OBJECTIVE
Students will view conferring with peers as a positive way to get and give helpful suggestions about writing.

TIME FRAME: 2–5 days
You may want to plan one day for students to assemble the Peer Conference Diary. Discussing its use, peer conference etiquette, and strategies for revising would follow on subsequent days.

ADVANCE PREPARATIONS

1. Cut two 6-by-9 inch pieces of construction paper for each student. They'll use the paper to make covers for the their Peer Conference Diaries.

2. Make five copies of the Peer Conference Summary form (page 46) for each student. This gives each student ten summary pages.

3. Optional:
   A. Prepare diaries ahead of time for younger students.

   B. Use staples rather than brads to bind the diaries. As students finish the first diary, they would make a new one rather than add pages.

4. Make a chart listing your peer conference rules (see page 33).

5. Designate an area for peer conferences (see page 56).

BACKGROUND
Revising involves students working together in peer conference groups, accepting constructive criticism, and making revision decisions. Obviously, this is not going to happen instantly. It requires a great deal of guidance and practice to develop and refine this important skill.

LITERATURE SUGGESTIONS
Individual or class stories

Lesson Outline

GUIDANCE
Remind students that the purpose of writing is to communicate an idea to other people. Because writers already understand what they are trying to say,

it is often difficult for them to see the places where their writing is unclear or needs more details. Therefore, in order to make their writing better, they confer with other people. These are people with whom the authors feel comfortable and who will give them honest, helpful ideas for making their writing better.

PEER CONFERENCE

1. Discuss your peer conference rules. Role-play ways to handle the following situations:

A. Choosing conference partners.

B. Saying "no" to a conference request.

C. Moving quietly to the area designated for conferring.

D. Thanking conference partners for their suggestions.

E. Returning to the work area and continuing with previous work.

Ask volunteers to role-play each situation. First, ask them to show the wrong way to handle the situation. Discuss how this behavior disrupts independent work time. Then have them show the correct way to handle the situation. Discuss.

2. Pass out the Peer Conference Summary forms and discuss how and when to complete each part. Give students directions for assembling these pages to make their Peer Conference Diaries. Explain that they will use the diaries to record their conferences. They will keep the Diaries in their Writing Folders.

3. Model a peer conference. To demonstrate the class rules for peer conferences, ask two volunteers to be your partners and then conduct a conference about your rough draft (from Skills lessons 5 to 7).

REVISING

4. Review the importance of revising. Every piece of writing can be revised in some way to make it more interesting or easier to understand. Model your revisions and explain your thinking.

One effective way to teach revising strategies is to use student examples as models. Ask a volunteer to share some of the suggestions his or her conference partners offered. Then have the student read and explain the resulting revisions. If possible, make a transparency of the student's writing as a visual aid.

There are several techniques that can make revising less tedious. First, be sure students are skipping lines as they write their rough drafts. This will enable them to make additions more easily. Second, be sure students are familiar with some common revision techniques. They should not take time to erase on rough drafts. Instead they should cross out unwanted words and use a caret to add words or phrases. Students will learn further revising and editing marks in Skills lesson 9.

Finally, if students need to add longer passages to their rough drafts, allow them to cut the rough drafts apart and use transparent tape to insert the passages where they belong. (You will need to model this technique.) These techniques will encourage students to concentrate on the revision process and not on the mechanics of revising.

PRACTICE

Have the class divide into peer conference groups and take turns discussing each member's rough draft. Take note of appropriate conference behaviors you observe. At the end of Independent Work time, share your observations with the class. In this way, you'll praise specific students and reinforce the desirability of these behaviors. Discuss appropriate ways to handle problem situations.

As groups finish, they will return to their desks to complete their diaries and begin making revisions.

EXTENSION ACTIVITY

Duplicate the Peer Conference Situation Cards (page 119). Mount these on construction paper or tagboard and laminate for durability. Divide the class into small groups. Give each group a situation card to role-play.

You can use this activity throughout the year to redirect inappropriate peer conference behavior in a positive way.

PEER CONFERENCE SITUATION CARDS

▼▼▼

CHOOSING PARTNERS

Pretend: You have finished writing your rough draft.

Act Out: How to read the rough draft quietly to yourself to check for words or ideas you might have left out.

How to get your Peer Conference Diary and fill it out.

How to ask classmates to be your conference partners.

SAYING "NO"

Pretend: You are busy working. A classmate asks you to be his conference partner, but you need to finish what you are doing.

Act Out: How to say "no" politely.

GOING TO A CONFERENCE

Pretend: You have agreed to be a conference partner.

Act Out: How to say "yes."

How to go to the conference area without disturbing others.

How to sit in a circle and get ready to listen.

THANKING PARTNERS

Pretend: You have finished your peer conference.

Act Out: How to thank your partners for giving you their honest opinions about your writing.

GETTING BACK TO WORK

Pretend: You have just thanked your conference partners.

Act Out: How conference partners return to their work quietly.

How you return to your desk and complete your Diary.

How you use the ideas you heard to make your story better.

Editing

OBJECTIVE

Students will recognize the need to edit their writing so that it conforms to standard spelling and punctuation.

TIME FRAME: 1–3 days

ADVANCE PREPARATIONS

1. You will be modeling the use of editing marks. Prepare a transparency of your rough draft or copy it on large chart paper. Be sure to include opportunities to make spelling, capitalization, and punctuation corrections.

2. Once my students have learned the writing-process skills, they work with parent volunteers on editing their projects. For this introductory lesson, however, I have the students work with peers. Plan your rules for peer editing. Will students work with one partner or with a small group? (I find that one partner is more efficient.) Will they work at their desks or at a special table? Will they make editing marks in pencil or use a special pen or marker? You may want to post these rules.

BACKGROUND

Do not expect your students to be able to perfectly edit their work. Instead, decide which skills they need to know most. Focus on one or two of these editing skills until your students are using them consistently. Then add a few more skills.

The Writing Process Pencil made in Skills lesson 3 has the most common editing marks mounted on the back of the Pencil. Refer students to this handy reference.

LITERATURE SUGGESTIONS

Individual or class stories

Lesson Outline

GUIDANCE

Write a short paragraph on the board. Do not use capital letters, punctuation marks, or spaces between words. Use lots of functional spellings. Ask students to read the paragraph. Discuss how standard spelling and punctuation make our writing easier to understand.

As you model the five-step editing

process below with your rough draft, teach common editing marks. Students can find these marks on the back of their Writing Process Pencil.

Students are already familiar with the 5-finger rule for choosing books. Now they will use their hand as a visual reminder of the five-step editing process.

1. Be sure there is a space between each word. (Hold up your hand and point to your thumb. Show students the large space between your thumb and fingers. This will help them remember the first step.)

2. Be sure each sentence ends with a period or other appropriate punctuation (question mark, exclamation mark, suspension points). Remind students that a sentence is a complete thought. This is a difficult concept for some students. Teach them how to read their stories slowly. When they feel themselves pausing or taking a short breath, they are usually at the end of a sentence. (Point to your index finger. Show students how someone might point this finger and say "stop." This will help them remember to stop their sentence with a period.)

3. After finding the end of each sentence, check to see that the word after the ending punctuation begins with a capital letter. (Point to your middle finger. Show students how this finger is taller

than the others. Capital letters are taller or bigger than lowercase letters.)

4. Make sure the specific names of people, pets, and places are capitalized. (Point to your ring finger. When someone has a ring on this finger, it may mean that the person is married. Remember the Mr. or Mrs. in front of their name. Ask students to use this clue to remind them that proper names and abbreviations are capitalized.)

5. Check spelling. Circle words that do not look correct. Use the spelling procedures taught in Skills lesson 5 to find the standard spellings. (Point to your last finger.)

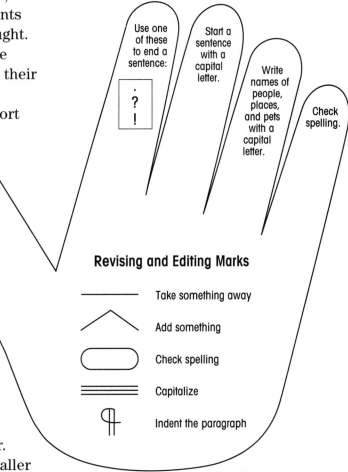

Revising and Editing Marks

——————	Take something away
⌃	Add something
⬭	Check spelling
≡	Capitalize
¶	Indent the paragraph

PRACTICE

Explain your class rules for peer editing. Then divide the class into peer editing groups of two to four students. While everyone in the editing group focuses on the same story, only the author writes the corrections on the rough draft.

After editing, students decide how much of their stories they want on each page of their books. (Remind students that they have already completed one of these pages in Skills lesson 5. Ask them to take this page out of their Writing Folders and use it as a model for planning their other pages.) An easy way to indicate a page break is to draw a vertical line after the last word to go on a page. Designate a special color for this line. Whatever color you choose, it should not be used anywhere else on the paper. This will make it more noticeable. (This is especially helpful if you will be having volunteers type students' stories. Every time they see a vertical red line, for example, they will know to begin a new page.)

EXTENSION ACTIVITY

Give students daily editing practice. Copy a short paragraph from your students' social studies or science textbook. You can put this on the board or on a transparency. As you write the paragraph, omit some capitals and punctuation marks. Misspell a few of the words that your students should know how to spell.

You may either discuss these errors at once or first ask students to recopy and edit the paragraph independently. If your students will be recopying the paragraph, be sure to keep it short. Remember that editing is already a difficult skill for many students. Avoid compounding that difficulty by having them recopy lengthy selections. (That is why I rely on parent volunteers to type out the final drafts of my students' Writing Projects.)

FIVE-STEP EDITING

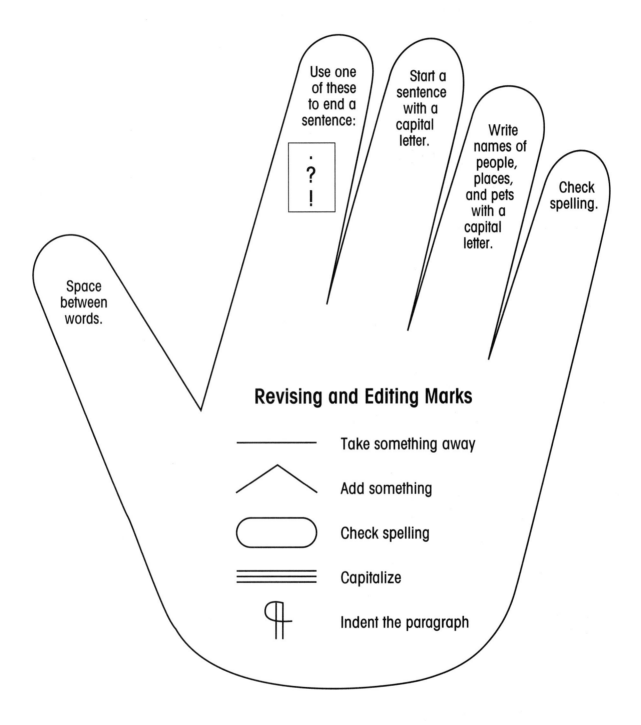

Use one of these to end a sentence:

.
?
!

Start a sentence with a capital letter.

Write names of people, places, and pets with a capital letter.

Check spelling.

Space between words.

Revising and Editing Marks

Take something away

Add something

Check spelling

Capitalize

Indent the paragraph

Layout and Publishing

OBJECTIVE

Students will become familiar with the parts of books and use this information to publish a window book.

TIME FRAME: 1–3 days

ADVANCE PREPARATIONS

1. Completely assemble your own window book. Save your rough draft.

2. Cut two pieces of 9-by-12-inch construction paper for each student's window book cover.

3. You may want to select a name for your class publishing company. Purchase an inexpensive ink stamp to use as your publishing company's logo. Keep this in your publishing area with an ink pad.

BACKGROUND

Following the completion of this lesson, students will be ready to begin working independently on self-selected writing projects. The tasks necessary to complete this writing process are sequenced on the writing arm of the Flow Chart (page 18). Relate each step of the writing process used in Skills lessons 4 through 10 to the corresponding task on the Flow Chart. Review your class rules for revising and editing, and make sure your students know where to find materials they will need for publishing.

Publishing gives students a genuine feeling of accomplishment, especially when students have been free to choose their own topics and plan the published format. Allow time for them to share their finished products with the class. You may want to periodically set aside a Literature Focus time for this purpose.

LITERATURE SUGGESTIONS

How a Book Is Made by Aliki

Lesson Outline

GUIDANCE

Read *How a Book Is Made* by Aliki. Then share your completed window book with your students. Remind them of the writing process steps you went through to get your book ready.

Compare your rough draft with your finished book.

Divide the class into groups of three to five students. Give each group several library books to examine. Ask them to look for different kinds of information authors include in their books.

Make a class list and discuss this information (title, author, copyright date, place of publication, dedication, etc.). Point out where each item should be located.

Students should also plan how they want their published books to look. They decide what size and kind of paper to use, and how their writing should appear on each page. (This page-by-page plan is called a *layout* or *dummy*.) Students began their layouts in Skills lesson 9 when they decided what should go on each page. Now they need to plan the title page, copyright page, and cover. For other books, they'll need to make decisions about picture placement. However, this project involves only one picture, the snapshot, which shows through a window on each page.

PRACTICE

1. Students make a layout, planning what will go on each page.

2. They trace and cut out a window page for each page of the book. They may use tablet paper, notebook paper, or unlined paper.

3. They recopy the rough draft on the window paper. (Or you may enlist volunteers to type the drafts.)

4. They cut a window on the front cover and then decorate around the cover. You may want to have students title the project "A Window On My World." If so, they may want to decorate around the cutout box to look like a window.

5. They assemble the pages and staple them in place. They glue or tape the snapshot in place on the inside of the back cover so that it shows through each page.

EXTENSION ACTIVITY

Throughout the year introduce the students to different publishing formats. In most cases, you will need to plan a whole class experience to teach the format. Then invite students to try it on their own. Keep a class list of possible publishing formats. These are some of the formats you may want to consider:

shape book	poetry
newspaper	pop-up book
poster	research report
ABC book	letter

1 (Daily Independent Work Task)

Writer's Journal

2 (Daily Independent Work Task)

Log In

3 (Daily Independent Work Task)

SQUIRT

(Reading)

4 (Daily Independent Work Task)

Log Out

5 (Daily Independent Work Task)

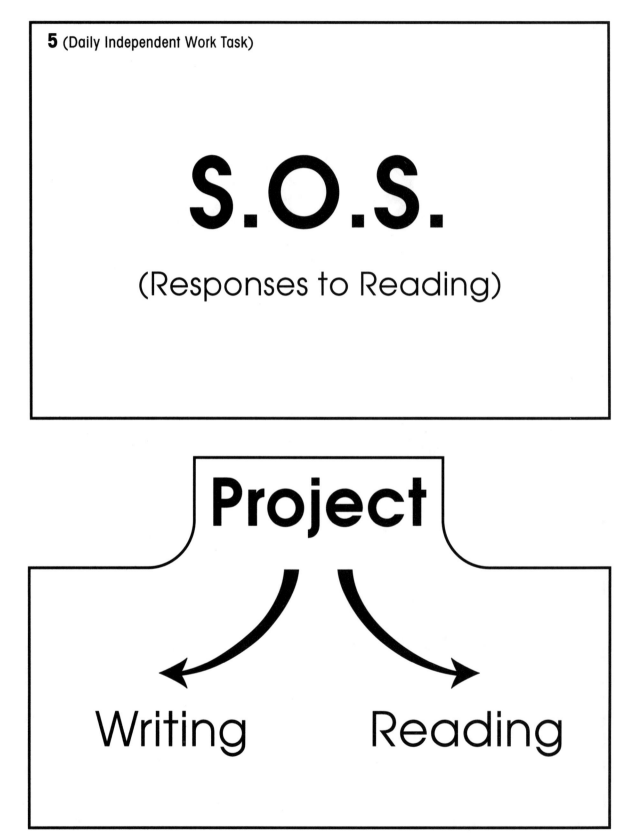

S.O.S.

(Responses to Reading)

Project

Writing   Reading

FLOW CHART BULLETIN BOARD PIECES

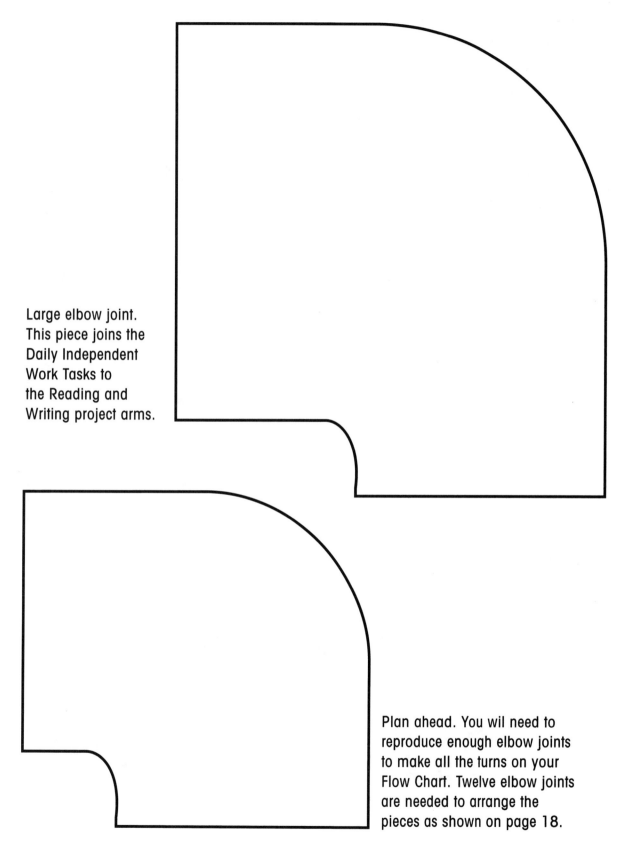

Large elbow joint. This piece joins the Daily Independent Work Tasks to the Reading and Writing project arms.

Plan ahead. You wil need to reproduce enough elbow joints to make all the turns on your Flow Chart. Twelve elbow joints are needed to arrange the pieces as shown on page 18.

1 (Writing Project Arm)

Story Map

2 (Writing Project Arm)

Rough Draft

3 (Writing Project Arm)

Peer Conference

4 (Writing Project Arm)

Revise

5 (Writing Project Arm)

Edit

3 (Writing Project Arm)

Layout

7 (Writing Project Arm)

Publish

1 (Reading Project Arm)

Choose a Book

2 (Reading Project Arm)

Read

3 (Reading Project Arm)

Make a Plan

4 (Reading Project Arm)

Peer Conference

5 (Reading Project Arm)

Revise

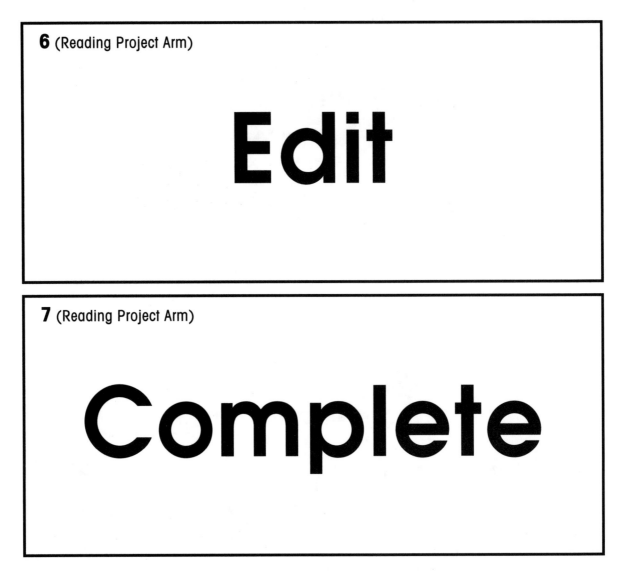

6 (Reading Project Arm)

Edit

7 (Reading Project Arm)

Complete

Bibliography

PROFESSIONAL BOOKS

Anderson, Richard C. et al. *Becoming a Nation of Readers: The Report of the Commission on Reading.* Champaign, IL: University of Illinois, Center for the Study of Reading, 1985.

Atwell, Nancy. *In the Middle: Writing, Reading, and Learning with Adolescents.* Portsmouth, NH: Heinemann, 1987.

Harste, Jerome C., Kathy G. Short, with Carolyn Burke. *Creating Classrooms for Authors: The Reading-Writing Connection.* Portsmouth, NH: Heinemann, 1988.

Holdaway, Don; Michael R. Sampson (ed.). *The Pursuit of Literacy: Early Reading and Writing.* Dubuque, IA: Kendall/Hunt, 1986.

Hornsby, David, Deborah Sukarnah, and Jo-Ann Parry. *Read On: A Conference Approach to Reading.* Portsmouth, NH: Heinemann, 1986.

Johnson, Terry D. and Daphne R. Louis. *Bringing It All Together: A Program for Literacy.* Portsmouth, NH: Heinemann, 1990.

Johnson, Terry D. and Daphne R. Louis. *Literacy Through Literature.* Portsmouth, NH: Heinemann, 1987.

Kobrin, Beverly. *Eyeopeners!* NY: Penguin Books, 1988.

Moen, Christine Boardman. *Teaching with Caldecott Books: Activities Across the Curriculum.* NY: Scholastic, 1991.

Parry, Jo-Ann and David Hornsby. *Write On: A Conference Approach to Writing.* Portsmouth, NH: Heinemann, 1985.

Routman, Regie. *Transitions from Literature to Literacy.* Portsmouth, NH: Heinemann, 1988.

SOURCES FOR CHILDREN'S LITERATURE

Hurst, Carol Otis. *A Long Time Ago. . . An Encyclopedia for Successfully Using Literature with Intermediate Readers.* Allen, TX: DLM, 1991.

Hurst, Carol Otis. *Once Upon a Time. . . Using Literature with Young Children.* Allen, TX: DLM, 1990.

Lima, Carolyn W. *A to Zoo: Subject Access to Children's Picture Books.* NY: Bowker, 1989.

CHILDREN'S BOOKS

Ahlberg, Janet and Allan Ahlberg. *The Jolly Postman.* Little, 1986.

Aliki. *How a Book Is Made.* Harper Collins, 1986.

Allard, Harry. *Miss Nelson is Missing.* Houghton, 1977.

Anderson, Joan. *Joshua's Westward Journal.* Morrow, 1987.

Avi. *Night Journeys.* Pantheon, 1979.

Berenstain, Jan and Stan. *The Berenstain Bears* series. Random House.

Blume, Judy. *Superfudge.* Dutton, 1980.

Brett, Jan. *Goldilocks and the Three Bears.* Sandcastle, 1990.

Briggs, Raymond. *Jim and the Beanstalk.* Putnam, 1980.

Burton, Virginia Lee. *Mike Mulligan and His Steam Shovel.* Houghton Mifflin, 1939.

Cleary, Beverly. *Ramona* books. Morrow.

Cleary, Beverly. *Ribsy.* Morrow, 1964.

Collier, James L. and Christopher Collier. *Jump Ship to Freedom.* Delacorte, 1981.

Ehrlich, Amy and Susan Jeffers. *Cinderella.* Dial, 1985.

Emberley, Barbara. *Drummer Hoff.* Prentice-Hall, 1967.

Flack, Marjorie. *The Story about Ping.* Scholastic, 1987.

Freeman, Don. *Corduroy.* Viking, 1968.

Fritz, Jean. *Brady.* Coward, 1960.

Fritz, Jean. *Shh! We're Writing the Constitution.* Putnam, 1987.

Galdone, Paul. *The Three Little Pigs.* Houghton, 1970.

Grimm, Jacob and Wilhelm. *Snow White.* Little, 1974.

Hall, Donald. *The Ox-Cart Man.* Viking, 1979.

Hoban, Lillian. *Arthur's Pen Pal.* Harper-Collins, 1976.

Hyman, Trina Schart. *Little Red Riding Hood.* Holiday, 1982.

Hyman, Trina Schart. *Sleeping Beauty*. Little, 1977.

Kellogg, Steven. *Best Friends*. Dial, 1986.

Kellogg, Steven. *The Island of the Skog*. Dial, 1976.

King-Smith, Dick. *Pigs Might Fly*. Viking, 1982.

Kipling, Rudyard. *Just So Stories*. Silver Burdett, 1987.

Kline, Suzy. *Herbie Jones*. Putnam, 1985.

Krauss, Ruth. *The Carrot Seed*. Scholastic, 1971.

Krensky, Stephen. *Who Really Discovered America?*. Hastings, 1987.

Lawson, Robert. *Ben and Me*. Little, 1939, 1988.

Lawson, Robert. *Captain Kidd's Cat*. Little, 1956, 1984.

Lionni, Leo. *Alexander and the Wind-Up Mouse*. Pantheon, 1969.

Lionni, Leo. *Fish Is Fish*. Pantheon, 1970.

Lionni, Leo. *Frederick*. Pantheon, 1967.

Lionni, Leo. *Swimmy*. Pantheon, 1963.

Lobel, Arnold. *Fables*. Harper Collins, 1980.

Lobel, Arnold. *Frog and Toad are Friends*. Harper Collins, 1970.

Lobel, Arnold. *A Treeful of Pigs*. Greenwillow, 1979.

MacLachlan, Patricia. *Sarah, Plain and Tall*. Harper Collins, 1985.

McCloskey, Robert. *Make Way for Ducklings*. Viking, 1941.

McDermott, Gerald. *Arrow to the Sun: A Pueblo Indian Tale*. Viking, 1974.

Minarik, Else Holmelund. *Little Bear*. Harper-Collins, 1957.

Munsch, Robert. *Moira's Birthday*. Annick, 1985.

Munsch, Robert. *The Paper Bag Princess*. Annick, 1980.

Murphy, Jim. *The Boys' War*. Houghton, 1990.

Murphy, Shirley Rousseau. *Tattie's River Journey*. Dial, 1983.

Numeroff, Laura Joffe. *If You Give a Mouse a Cookie: The Diary of a Church Mouse*. Atheneum, 1987.

Parish, Peggy. *Amelia Bedelia*. Scholastic, 1970.

Peet, Bill. *Chester the Worldly Pig*. Houghton, 1965.

Pinkwater, Daniel Manus. *The Big Orange Splot*. Scholastic, 1981.

Rylant, Cynthia. *When I Was Young in the Mountains*. Dutton, 1982.

Scieszka, Jon. *The True Story of the 3 Little Pigs*. Viking Kestrel, 1989.

Sendak, Maurice. *Where the Wild Things Are*. Scholastic, 1986.

Seuss, Dr. *Green Eggs and Ham*. Random House, 1960.

Sleator, William. *The Angry Moon*. Little, 1970.

Speare, Elizabeth George. *The Sign of the Beaver*. Houghton, 1983.

Steig, William. *Amos and Boris*. Penguin, 1971/1977.

Steig, William. *Roland the Minstrel Pig*. Windmill Books, 1968.

Steptoe, John. *Mufaro's Beautiful Daughters*. Scholastic, 1987.

Stevenson, Robert Louis. *Treasure Island*. Many versions.

Taylor, Mark. *Henry the Explorer*. Atheneum, 1976.

Turkle, Brinton. *Deep in the Forest*. Dutton, 1976.

Van Allsburg, Chris. *The Polar Express*. Houghton, 1985.

Van Allsburg, Chris. *Jumanji*. Houghton, 1981.

Viorst, Judith. *Alexander and the Terrible, Horrible, No Good, Very Bad Day*. Macmillan, 1987.

Viorst, Judith. *Alexander, Who Used to Be Rich Last Sunday*. Atheneum, 1978.

Viorst, Judith. *If I Were in Charge of the World and Other Worries*. Atheneum, 1981.

Viorst, Judith. *Rosie and Michael*. Atheneum, 1974.

Williams, Vera B. *Three Days on a River in a Red Canoe*. Greenwillow, 1981.

Williams, Vera B. and Jennifer Williams. *Stringbean's Trip to the Shining Sea*. Greenwillow, 1988.

Wiseman, B. *Morris the Moose Goes to School*. Scholastic, 1970.

Yolen, Jane. *Sleeping Ugly*. Coward, 1981.

Yorinks, Arthur. *Hey, Al*. Farrar, 1986.

Young, Ed. *Lon Po Po*. Philomel, 1989.